**Narrow
Gauge
the
World Over**

Narrow Gauge the World Over

PATRICK WHITEHOUSE
and PETER ALLEN

LONDON
IAN ALLAN LTD

First published 1976

ISBN 0 7110 0600 8-100/74

© Patrick Whitehouse and Peter Allen 1976

Published by Ian Allan Ltd, Shepperton, Surrey,
and printed by Ian Allan Printing Ltd.

Contents

Introduction

Another railway picture book? Yes indeed, for the time has come, we think, to take a look back over twenty-five years at narrow gauge rail around the world and at steam in particular from the viewpoint of the seventies. At the end of this decade steam will all be gone except perhaps where guarded by dedicated amateurs or in some remote hill fastness in Spain or possibly in its last lingering death throes in India or Africa or behind the Iron Curtain.

In countries like Japan, New Zealand and South Africa — all Africa in fact except the northern coastal strip — where the narrow gauge is the national standard, the same processes are at work today as you find in the wider gauge world. Electrification and diesel power are coming in and steam, despite a fine rearguard action in southern Africa, is in retreat. Now steam in Japan is virtually all gone; in New Zealand there is none left in the north island and precious little in the south. Southern Africa is a more fertile field; the Republic itself is still well populated with nearly 2,000 steam survivors; so are Angola and Rhodesia, the homes of the Garratts. This also applies to Mozambique, where recently we found steam engines of twenty-seven different types and there are, in fact, several hundred all told.

In India, where broad gauge and metre gauge both operate, there is still plenty of steam and the last steam locomotives have only just been built. But although the oil crisis has kept steam alive, more and more diesel power is being constructed and locally too. Ceylon has a 2ft 6in gauge line using 1929-built Hunslet tanks, as well as Krupp diesels.

The Argentine metre gauge network is on diesel power now and also those of Chile and Brazil, but one of us found a rich lode of ore in Bolivia and a fascinating coal line in Patagonia as late as 1967, so you never can be quite certain.

So while the big narrow gauge networks which serve whole provinces or nations have moved inexorably towards the end of steam, what of the hundreds of little lines — the feeder lines, the local lines, the mountain lines, the tourist lines, the industrial lines — on narrow gauge: how have they fared in the past seven years and how can they look forward in the seventies?

With anxiety and fear, we are sure, for they have been falling fast. The more prosperous or essential lines, like those serving the industrial areas of northern Spain for example, will survive but under diesel power; a few others serving coal fields may continue with steam for a few years. Portugal, another country in reach of most of us, still runs some narrow gauge passenger trains with sparkling 2-4-6-0 Mallet tanks carrying copper-capped chimneys. Those systems are worth a visit but to catch steam it will have to be soon. Steam can still be found in Austria on the Zillertal and also on the Styrian Government line as well as in the north near to the Czech border. In some places where a new diesel outfit cannot be afforded, decaying steam will hang on, but the difficulty and expense of getting spares, especially boilers, is becoming more and more pressing. And in all places the building of roads and the cheapness and convenience of motor cars and trucks bring death to the little narrow gauge lines. Paradoxically, where they do manage to survive, as in the backwoods lines in India for example, steam often survives too.

Where then can we look for a little sunshine? First and foremost among the lines revived and operated by enthusiasts to attract the tourists. The Talyllyn, the pioneer preservationist-operated railway, and the Festiniog are both flourishing; the Welshpool and Llanfair is jogging its gentle way along the Banwy Valley; the Isle of Man railway is trying but has far to go; the Vale of Rheidol will find supporters if British Rail decides to throw its hand in — though the danger here is that they may run it to death first. Abroad, in slightly different style, the societies and groups of narrow gauge enthusiasts attract the crowds. 'Puffing Billy' outside Melbourne is one, the Durango to Silverton branch of the Denver and Rio Grande is another, and since July 1971 a weekend public service has been run on a 64 mile section of the abandoned Durango to Alamosa line. This together with nine locomotives and 130 cars was rescued by the state and trains run between Antonito, Colorado, and Chama, New Mexico, over the Cumbres Pass. The East Broad Top is a third, and the Edaville, beloved by the late Nelson Blount, continues to give joy rides round the cranberry bogs of Cape Cod. Of these the 'Puffing Billy' line is still state-owned though enthusiast-operated and the former D&RGW was saved simply by tourist demand; it now carries around 100,000 passengers annually and runs two trains daily over the 90 mile return journey in the high season. These and many others like the Swiss railway out of Vevey with its German Mallet and ex-Réseau Breton tanks, the French Chemins de Fer Touristiques and similar lines set up in Germany and Scandinavia depend first and foremost on dedicated, hardworking enthusiasts — people who refuse to take no for an answer. There is also tough work needing those who will slave like Brunel's "considerable body of navigators" on clearing scrub and re-laying track for no pay. These new amateur-professionals have learned to run the finished working system in an orderly and professional way. But for these happy people these lines would fail, but those which succeed, and several have succeeded beyond the wildest dreams of their sponsors, have earned the support, yes and the respect too, of a large public and are now recognised tourist attractions. Think of it: the Festiniog, which was derelict twenty years ago, carried nearly 400,000 passengers in 1974 and made a profit, and this in proportion applies also to the other Welsh narrow gauge lines. The Great Little Trains of Wales they are indeed.

If we look back now these past twenty-five years, what a rich scene the narrow gauge has presented — gigantic 4-8-4s for express passenger and freight service in South Africa and New Zealand and some others, designed by the great Chapelon himself, in Brazil; a huge family of Garratts in South Africa, Rhodesia, Angola and Kenya; a metre gauge network in India larger than that of the broad gauge, with burnished red passenger engines together with a host of 2ft 6in and 2ft gauge lines; the Japanese National Railways with big stoker-fired 2-8-4s and 4-6-4s and many of graceful Pacifics;

in the USA a big but disintegrating mountain system on 3ft gauge in Colorado whose 2-8-2 all-rounders were slightly bigger than the Stanier 2-8-0s on the LMS: all over East Asia metre gauge in profusion, except where some alien thinking had introduced 3ft 6in. The biggest Garratts of all working in Kenya — and there was most of South America to add to this with some powerful rack engines for the Andes, and main line and long distance haulage in the Argentine and Brazil. Australia too had its main line systems: all of Queensland with its charming green-boilered Pacifics and light blue suburban tanks, some of South Australia with some strong 3ft 6in Garratts, and Western Australia with its graceful British-built green engines.

This then is what the main line narrow gauge systems had to offer, and what a rich feast it was. We hope to have succeeded in illustrating some of these scenes, big-time rail-roading all of them, in one way or another, either in the terrain they worked in, or in sheer slogging length of run, in the loads lifted or the intensive service they provided.

It is when we turn to the little lines, the feeder lines, the secondary systems, the mountain roads and the coal-haulers that the incredible variety and colour of the narrow gauge world present themselves. There is a legion of different systems and different gauges from 4ft 8in on the Mount Washington Cog Railway (which makes this centenarian technically narrow gauge and thus allows it into this book) to 1ft 3in at Ravenglass and and New Romney; metre and 3ft 6in make up most of the mileage with 3ft, 760mm (2ft 6in) and 750mm in close support, but there was a fair mileage of 600mm, or 2ft near enough, and some odd gauges like 4ft and 3ft 7½in in Spain with 95mm and 105mm around the Mediterranean.

The locomotives on these smaller systems are of every type and wheel arrangement. Tender engines of some size have been used from time to time, like the Pacifics and 2-10-0s from Tunis that went to the Robla line in Spain, and also there, Garratts and Mallets on the Sierra Menera iron ore line. Mexico too had some big Mallets at one time and a long-lived group of Baldwin tender engines including the last two 4-4-0s built in America, the ancestral home of this type, dating from 1945. The White Pass and Yukon had some sizeable 2-8-2s for the 3ft gauge and so did the East Broad Top for hauling coal in Pennsylvania. In South America the secondary metre gauge systems of the Argentine had some substantial Pacifics and Mikados and the huge Esslingen 0-12-2 rack engines. Big Japanese-built 2-10-2s have been introduced in the last few years on the 3ft 6in gauge coal lines in the Argentine, some of which run on the isolated Rio Turbio line near the Straits of Magellan, the most southerly railway in the world. The last Atlantics in the world were hunted down on the 3ft 6in lines of Mozambique by both of the authors as late as 1974 and found to be in good heart.

But it is of course the tank engines which show the greatest variety; every imaginable builder in every country has contributed some and a few even have been home made — Kitson, Henschel, Fives-Lille, Tubize, Mitsubishi, Baldwin, Maquinista, Montreal Locomotive, Nydqvist & Holm, Breda, Swiss Locomotive, and a dozen others and more have contributed engines over the years, in sizes from five tons to a hundred. Apart from special monsters for the rack, the big German 2-10-2s probably led the tank engine parade, perhaps

followed by the Lough Swilly's great 4-8-4s and by Mallets like the improbable Henschel 2-4-6-0s for Portugal, or the double 0-6-0s of France. After that almost every imaginable wheel arrangement, short of single drivers, could be found in the last twenty-five years, though offhand we cannot recall a 4-4-4. 0-6-0s, 2-6-2s and 0-6-2s, these last usually of German origin, abounded and 2-8-2s, 2-6-0s and elegant 4-4-0s and 4-6-0s were plentiful. A couple of Shay geared engines came to light in Bolivia in 1967 and some Kitson-Meyer rack engines survived into the sixties in Chile.

Some preposterous-looking rack engines have enlivened this period, of which the oddest are probably those on the magnificent Mount Washington Cog Railway which runs on a really steep Riggenbach ladder; these are still in service and so are those strange praying-mantis machines on the Achensee Bahn and Schneeberg lines in Austria. Alas, the Fell centre-rail lines in New Zealand and also the one in Brazil have gone so the last in the world on this system are the Snaefell Mountain Railway in the Isle of Man and the similar electrified line near Chamonix in France.

Other railways in the mountains are still with us; the future of the Darjeeling 2ft gauge railway was obscure after the multiple damage it suffered in the unprecedented monsoon storms of 1968 but it is back again and going strong. So is the rack line in the Nilgiri hills in southern India.

These scenes we think are well worth recording, although we made a similar study nine years ago. Much fresh material has come to hand since then and new information is constantly reaching us, even though most of this is like the bad news of the death of an old friend; now and again the failing firelight flickers up with some good tidings, a line restored to use by some enthusiasts' group, some steam engines built for export by Esslingen or Hitachi, a closure reprieved or a service restored. These changes and a wealth of new pictures, hardly any of which have ever been published before, are the raison d'être of this book. It follows closely the pattern of our earlier collaboration *Round the World on the Narrow Gauge* published in 1966. This time of course the book has a more backward look but many pictures date from the last eight or ten years and of these many show scenes still visible today. This time we have changed the format slightly to allow more pictures and less formal script. Instead, we have used fairly lengthy and descriptive captions which we think serve the purpose of our scrapbook, for that is what it is, rather better.

Our only regret is that costs have prohibited the wide use of colour. Some very attractive colours have illuminated the narrow gauge in the past quarter century. Pride of place must go to the emerald green tank engines of the Economic Railways of Asturias, with their burnished brass and copper fittings, but the crimson engines of Kenya run them close; the spotless green of the Festiniog, the Indian red or the light blue of Indian locomotives would look well in colour reproduction and so would those glorious old coaches on the Talylln.

However, black and white must rule and we can only console ourselves that we have got some contributions from the masters, Harold Navé, O. Winthur Laursen, Gerry Best, Jim Shaughnessy, Lawrence Marshall, Trevor Rowe, Derek Cross, Frank Barry and Allen Jorgensen, among many others.

The form of the book, geographically divided rather than by any more obscure arrangement, we hope will be intelligible and acceptable.

Great Britain and Ireland

The past quarter century has seen a revolution in transport matters, and somewhat naturally the old, slow-moving anachronistic narrow gauge railways have gone, for they had no place in today's world which is not attuned to life without a motor car. To the railway student and enthusiast this is of course a pity, for each line in its own way was charming enough, not only from the railway point of view but also for the fact that the search for these lines often took us into quiet, undeveloped countryside where life, even in the 1950s, was relatively unsophisticated and without the now ubiquitous petrol pump. Life may have been a little slower, but it was good to live.

The change has probably been most apparent in Ireland, certainly as far as the narrow gauge railway is concerned, for twenty-five years ago these little lines were scattered over a fair proportion of the country, particularly in the north and south-west. In those days you could still go by corridor train, in Derby-built London Midland & Scottish Railway maroon-coloured coaches, from Ballymoney to Ballycastle behind a Worsdell von Borries compound 2-4-2 tank; trains of cattle and coal worked in abundance over the Cavan and Leitrim section of Eire's Great Southern Railway, and a daily freight train was aping the antics of a Kerry goat over the Sleive Mish mountains between Tralee and Dingle. The rot began with the coal famine of 1947 and continued through the fifties until the last train on Ireland's narrow gauge railways ran on the, by then, fully dieselised West Clare line on September 27th, 1960. But that first decade of our period was full of adventure. You could travel on a red and cream County Donegal train all the way from Londonderry to Killybegs or Ballyshannon on the far west coast, and part of the journey would be behind big 4-6-4 or 2-6-4 geranium red tank engines, and if you took the Letterkenny branch you could cross over at the terminus and find the Lough Swilly's gleaming black tank engines with their polished brasswork waiting to take you back to 'Derry in the wooden-seated bogie coach at the rear of a freight train. The West Clare too was running steam with ageing 0-6-2, 2-6-2 and 4-6-0 tank engines which were so run down that the engines from the ailing Tralee and Dingle line were brought in to supplement them. One could go on, but today this is all just a memory reinforced by photographs and if one is lucky,

perhaps a little film — apart from these it scarcely seems possible that such lines ever existed at all.

Back in Britain the narrow gauge had almost ceased in England, was gone in Scotland, and just limping along in Wales. The survivor in England was the Ashover in Derbyshire and this, together with its World War I veteran Baldwin 2-6-2 tanks, succumbed in 1950. In Wales the picture was a little brighter, but to those with eyes to see, the end of the story as it had been for seventy-five years was nearly reached. In 1946 the well-known Festiniog Railway ran its final freight train on August 2nd, thus bringing to an end almost three-quarters of a century of steam on its narrow gauge. One by one the other relatively numerous narrow gauge lines dwindled down — the Corris in 1948, the Talyllyn in 1950, and the Welshpool and Llanfair section of British Railways in 1956. Strangely enough, it was a major British railway, the Great Western, which re-opened its Vale of Rheidol section of 2ft gauge line to passengers in 1945, and led the way to change.

This change was really a revolution, and its story is too well known today to bear much repetition. Suffice it to say that the 2ft 3in gauge Talyllyn line, based at Towyn in Merioneth, was saved by a preservation society, and through sheer faith and hard work was reborn as a tourist line. This was followed by the revival of the Festiniog Railway in 1955, and the Welshpool and Llanfair in 1963, under similar circumstances. In 1970, after dilly-dallying and wanting to abandon its Vale of Rheidol line BR at last realised its possibilities, and has even set up a supporters' association (non-voting!) to assist it.

So the majority of the little lines which were operating in the United Kingdom in 1945 are still safe, though carrying vastly different traffic from the slate and merchandise of their origin. They are seasonal lines only, but all told they carry around half a million passengers a year. The amateurs have become the new professionals.

There are few other lines worthy of mention — the Snowdon Mountain cog railway is still going strong, and very popular in spite of its necessarily high fares, and the 3ft gauge line in the Isle of Man, closed as uneconomic by its former owners, still runs steam between Port Erin and Castletown. The rest of the network has been torn up, after disastrous experiments in running steam tourist trains over the whole system. Two other lines of note have gone — the Penrhyn Quarry Railway, and the Dinorwic Quarry Railway — the latter had not only a 2ft gauge line but a 4ft gauge one too. These are, we fear, natural casualties in this day and age, but many of their engines survive. Some are in private hands and can be seen operating at places like Alan Bloom's Bressingham Gardens, and the Festiniog Railway runs two of the Penrhyn's 'main line' engines, *Linda* and *Blanche*.

On the whole it is a pretty satisfactory position.

Above: The Penrhyn Slate Quarries in their hey-day had a large family of 0-4-0 tank engines, most of which worked up at the quarry galleries high up on the mountain side. Here is *Winifred* outside the works. She was built by Hunslet in 1885.

Right: The ironstone mines in the Midlands of England had an extraordinary variety of little railways including standard, 3ft 6in, metre and 3ft gauges. The photograph shows the Kettering Furnaces Railway with one of their 0-4-0 3ft gauge engines. These charming nineteenth century scenes were still visible as recently as 1960. The locomotive was built by Black Hawthorn and goes back to the last century.

Far right: Pike Bros, Fayle & Co Ltd operated a 2ft 8in gauge line from Furzebrook Clay Mines near Wareham in Dorset. Their engines carried no numbers but nameplates of Latin numbers. Here is *Quintus* taking a rest in the Oak Woods near Oakcreech Grange in August 1954. *Quintus* was built by Manning Wardle in 1914.

Above: Guinness's Brewery in Dublin in the early 1960s was a fine place for small-gauge steam engines. Here with some fierce curves and furious gradients the little 0-4-0 tank engines of Mr Geoghegan, with their amazingly compact design, ran around for years. One is mercifully preserved in the Guinness Museum in Dublin and another at the Narrow Gauge Museum at Towyn. When some motive power was wanted for shunting on Guinness's broad gauge lines, one of these little engines could be loaded into a special wagon which it then drove through a friction-gear and was thus able to operate on the 5ft 3in gauge. This remarkable contrivance is shown in the picture.

Above right: The Bowater Paper Mills at Sittingbourne in North Kent operated an attractive 2ft 6in gauge railway not only for freight purposes between Ridham Dock and the works but also for passengers to and from the various points inside the works fence. For this purpose a wide variety of locomotives was used of which the newest, the 0-4-4-0 *Monarch,* has now gone to the Welshpool & Llanfair Light Railway in Wales and four others have gone to Whipsnade Zoo. Bowaters decided to close the line but the Locomotive Club of Great Britain have been able to take over the running of this

railway for enthusiasts with some of the surviving 0-4-2 and 0-6-2 locomotives. Here is a typical freight train on the Bowater line with one of their 0-6-2 tanks *Superior.*

Right: The Ravenglass & Eskdale Railway runs through some beautiful hilly country in Cumberland and, although this is rather more a miniature railway than a narrow gauge line, it nevertheless deserves inclusion if only for this picture of 0-8-2 *River Mite* approaching Irton Road Station with a train of open coaches in high summer.

Far right: Quite different from the Ravenglass & Eskdale is the 15in gauge Romney, Hythe & Dymchurch which runs across Romney Marsh from Hythe through to Dungeness. This railway, built in 1925 has just been bought up by a group of enthusiasts got together by Mr Bill McAlpine. The Romney, Hythe & Dymchurch has always used magnificent near-scale models of full-size engines. Here are two of them at Hythe Station: Pacific No 2 *Highland Chief* in what one might call the Gresley LNER style, and Canadian Pacific type 4-6-2 No 10 *Dr Syn.* This picture shows the whole scene excellently. Half close your eyes and they look like full-scale locomotives.

12

Right: The decision of the Isle of Man Railway to close its operations caused a considerable turmoil in 1966. However, a new organisation has taken over the running of the line and, while it has its problems, there is hope that part of the railway may manage to survive as a tourist and holiday attraction. It certainly deserves to for some of its rolling stock is really delightful. Here is a picture of 2-4-0 Beyer Peacock tank engine No 11 *Maitland* arriving at Crosby with a children's excursion.

Far right: The Manx Electric Railway running from Douglas along the coast to Ramsey has been a holiday attraction for many years. It runs on the 3ft gauge and is a must for all narrow gauge enthusiasts, as is the 3ft 6in gauge electric line up to Snae Fell Mountain with the Fell centre-rail for braking. Here is motor coach No 1 at Douglas with a nice old Baldwin 'toast-rack' coach in tow.

Below: The pioneer enthusiasts' railway in Wales—indeed in all Britain and the whole world—is the Talyllyn which was salvaged from a derelict condition by a group of enthusiasts led by L.T.C. Rolt and is now a flourishing concern for summer visitors. This little line runs on the 2ft 3in gauge and has an attractive variety of locomotives to supplement its two originals dating from 1865. Here is a train between Towyn and the mountains just beyond Pendre, the first station out, double-headed with 0-4-0 tank No 6 *Douglas* and 0-4-2 tank No 4 *Edward Thomas.*

Below right: British Railways have continued to run the 2ft gauge line between Aberystwyth and Devil's Bridge through all the vicissitudes of postwar railway operation. As far as we know, this arrangement will continue for the next few years under this ownership. The line runs through some supremely beautiful country and has the attraction of operating the last three live steam locomotives on British Railways, a family of 2-6-2 tanks. The picture shows No 7 *Owain Glyndŵr* at Aberystwyth. At the time the picture was taken in 1960 the locomotive was in lined-out British Railways green, but her present-day livery is now the standard blue.

Second in the preservation field in Wales to get going was the Festiniog. This was rescued from a derelict condition by a group of enthusiasts led by Alan Pegler, who was once the proud owner of the *Flying Scotsman*. The Festiniog is the daddy of them all as far as its original date is concerned, as it goes back to the horse drawn days of the early part of last century and in 1863 it became the first narrow gauge steam railway in the world. One of its original locomotives *Prince* still survives, though how much of the original engine is in existence is rather like asking how much remains of a favourite cricket bat which has had three new blades and five new handles. Be that as it may, two of the original double Fairlie engines survive, one being *Merddin Emrys* and the other *Taliesin*, now named *Earl of Merioneth* in honour of the Duke of Edinburgh, though the latter is now out to grass. One photograph (*above*) depicts the 'Earl' coming out of the cutting at Gysfa whilst the other (*above right*) shows *Merddin Emrys* at Tan-y-Bwlch during the Centenary of Steam celebrations in 1963.

There is a third enthusiasts' railway in Wales: the Welshpool and Llanfair which operates the old Great Western, formerly Cambrian, 2ft 6in gauge line between Lysfaen and Llanfair Caereinion. The line owns five steam engines, including one from Austria as well as one from the sugar lines of Antigua, and two 0-6-0 tank engines, *The Earl* and the *Countess* built by Beyer Peacock in 1903. The pictures show (*right*) *The Earl* and (*far right*) the *Countess* and her reflection. These four engines are reinforced by *Monarch* from Bowater Paper Mills, (not in use) and some coaches also from the Zillertal Railway in Austria.

Above: On the borders of Wales near the Shropshire boundary was a little country line called the Snailbeach & District Railway. This line, surviving until shortly after the war, just comes into our period. The photograph shows Snailbeach shed in 1943 with Kerr Stuart 0-4-2 tank engine No 2 outside the shed and two Baldwin 4-6-0 World War I tanks inside.

Above right: The Padarn Railway had 2ft gauge locomotives up in the Dinorwic quarries but at Llanberis the slate was transferred in its trucks on to special 4ft gauge wagons and hauled down to the coast to Port Dinorwic on this very rare gauge. We are glad to have a picture of the 4ft gauge train with pig-a-back wagons loaded with 2ft gauge trucks. The 4ft gauge was unusual but not unique, as it turns up in Spain on the Tharsis line and also on the Glasgow underground. A 2ft gauge line has now been constructed on part of the old 4ft road operated as a tourist attraction by a new group of enthusiasts under the name of the Llanberis Lake Railway with three Hunslet 0-4-0 tanks.

Right: Another line which barely survived the war was the Ashover Railway — it had a precarious freight service until the late 1940s and, as shown in the photograph above, was persuaded in 1947 to hitch up some open wagons to let enthusiasts of the Birmingham Locomotive Club take a ride on it. The Baldwin 4-6-0 is *Peggy,* the last of her clan.

Far right: Linda, Blanche and *Charles* were the Penrhyn Quarry's 'Main Line' engines. They were used exclusively on the railway between the quarry proper and Port Penrhyn on the Menai Strait. Now that the Penrhyn lines are all closed, *Charles* rests in the Industrial Railway Museum at the Castle whilst his sisters *Linda* and *Blanche* are hard at work on the Festiniog.

Above left: Until the early 1950s there was still a considerable mileage of 3ft gauge railway in the north of Ireland. Some of this belonged to the NCC (later the Ulster Transport Authority) running between Ballymena and Larne and from Ballymoney to Ballycastle. This picture shows one of the 2-4-2 two-cylinder Worsdell Von Borries compounds on the Ballycastle line in 1950 after the state had taken over lines from the NCC. These were attractive little engines and they also performed very well.

Above: The Londonderry & Lough Swilly Railway did not survive beyond 1953 as a railway though the company continues to operate bus and lorry fleets under that name. Originally the line ran from Londonderry to the far west at Burtonport right across County Donegal with an additional branch to Buncrana. The Lough Swilly was always an attractive railway with a wide variety of dark green engines including two 4-8-0 tender engines, two huge 4-8-4 tanks and a number of 4-6-2 and 4-6-0 tanks as well. Here is a freight train in 1952 at Newtoncunningham with 4-6-0T No 3 at the head.

The County Donegal Railways Joint Committee operated a large network of 3ft gauge lines in the north-west of Ireland. It was the first line to make use of the economical railcar and since the 1930s all regular passenger traffic was handled by these sturdy red and cream 'rail buses'. This car originally came from the late lamented Clogher Valley Tramway and is seen here (*far left*) coming through the wild Barnesmore Gap in 1954. On high days and holidays the County Donegal was ready and anxious to put on excursions to the coast at Ballyshannon. Two trains were generally run, one from Strabane and a second from Stranorlar. This sometimes meant running up to tremendous lengths, taxing the powerful 2-6-4 and 4-6-4 tank engines to the utmost. The picture (*left*) shows the sad scene of the last excursion on the County Donegal climbing up from the coast through the Barnesmore Gap with cherry-red tank engine *Blanche* at the head and no less than eleven coaches behind her on August Bank Holiday Monday 1959.

Above left: In the centre of
Ireland was the 3ft gauge Cavan
and Leitrim Railway (part of CIE)
kept alive by the coal deposits at
Arigna which supplemented the
very small and sporadic
agricultural traffic until 1959.
This picture here shows one of
the 4-4-0 tanks, built for this line,
at Dromod. They also dealt with
most of the coal traffic down the
Arigna Tramway branch though
as they became worn out their
place was taken by ex-Tralee and
Dingle 2-6-0 tanks.

Above: The Cavan and Leitrim
also obtained locomotives from
other parts of Ireland besides
2-6-0 and 2-6-2 tank engines
from the Tralee and Dingle such
as the 2-4-2s of the Cork
Blackrock and Passage Railway.
Here is 2-6-0 tank No 6T from
the Tralee and Dingle on the last
days of working on the C&L. The
coaches are just about on their
last legs. Again the scene is at
Dromod.

Left: Here on the Cavan and
Leitrim is an attractive view on
the Erne Viaduct at Belturbet
showing a mixed train with one
of the Tralee and Dingle engines,
No 4, a 2-6-0 built by Kerr Stuart
in 1903.

Above: The Tralee and Dingle 3ft gauge Railway in County Kerry kept going after the war by dint of running a livestock train once a month down from Dingle Market to Tralee. This was a considerable task for the road was mountainous and hard and the trains had to accommodate something like twenty cattle wagons at once. In high summer the task was harder and the very limited motive power was divided up between a double-headed 20-van train, and a single-headed 10-van train as the maximum load for one engine was 11 vans. The picture shows two of the T&D 2-6-0 tanks wrestling with the first section of the 1 in 30 climb up to the summit at Glenagalt. Glenagalt is the 'Glen of the Mad' where it is said there was a spring which cured insanity and also that on the Day of Judgement all the mad dead of Ireland will gather for their special part in the ceremonies.

Above right: One of the most attractive little lines in the Irish Republic was the Schull and Skibbereen Railway in the west of Co Cork. It had two attractive 4-4-0 tank locomotives with a third engine, of a type which is very unusual on the narrow gauge, an 0-4-4T. This originally worked on the Cork and Muskerry but ended up by doing most of the donkey-work on the S&S before it closed down. She is shown at Skibbereen in 1950 and was built by T. Green & Son in 1893.

Right: The West Clare Railway in Ireland between Ennis, Kilkee and Kilrush also survived into the 1950s and then collapsed. It passed through a singularly wild and open stretch of the coastal area of County Clare and some furious and fierce gales of wind would frequently beset the train. Here is a train at Milltown Malbay in 1951 with 4-6-0 tank No 3 built by Hunslet.

The Mainland of Europe

As sophistication and the motor car have become commonplace in Europe, so the narrow gauge railway as a means of transport has declined: and those lines which survive do so generally on a subsidy or as some form of tourist business. There has been a tremendous change in the pattern over the past quarter century, a change which has accelerated rapidly during the last decade. World War II and the ravages of armies wrought considerable havoc, particularly in France where a once huge network was very considerably reduced — there was a time when except for a few miles you could, with many changes, get from the Channel to the Mediterra-

nean via the narrow gauge: then, as the countries of Europe pulled themselves out of the aftermath of war the narrow gauge system retreated, as it were, into the hills and the country districts where it provided the only reasonable means of transport. But even here it has been attacked either by road progress or by the converting of the narrow gauge tracks into standard gauge, as has been done with part of the once huge Reseau Breton network in France — a system once thought by many to be secure. Now, apart from lines in Eastern Europe and some enthusiast preservations steam has almost disappeared. The advent of the postwar railcar era has certainly stayed the execution in many cases, but the inevitable end has only been staved off.

One of the saving graces of the European narrow gauge railways has been the continental Concession system. This operates by handing the section of line concerned over to a private or local authority concern on an agreed repairing lease (often rent free) and thus giving the Concessionaires an incentive to provide as efficient and economical a transport service as possible. One advantage of this system is that it goes a long way to ensure and encourage an active local management, which know the peculiarities of the area — good business practice in every sense. The Concessionary system applies particularly in France, Germany and Italy. Examples could be found in the French CFD concern, which operated part of the SNCF system (and took up to half of any savings achieved), and the German Westfälische Landeseisenbahn. On all these lines economy is the watchword coupled with an encouragement to obtain any traffic in the offing. It all works very much on the lines of the British privately-owned tourist lines, where the driver is the fitter in the winter and the guard doubles up as a shunter, ticket collector and booking clerk when required. An excellent example of this is on the Regentalbahn in Germany, where the driver of the 0-6-0 tank is the same chap who drives the bus when the train is not running that particular trip!

But it is to Eastern Europe that the enthusiast has turned in recent years, particularly to Jugoslavia, Bulgaria and Romania, where the narrow gauge lines are still superb, not only in their motive power but their scenery too. These sections are disappearing rapidly as roads and the standard gauge take over, but even now there is plenty to see, though the sight and sound of a double-headed train climbing its way out of Visegrad up to the spiral tunnels en route to Titovo Uzicé is now literally something out of this world. The railcars (very comfortable) are taking over, and diesels increase but steam still operates over part of the narrow gauge main line in Jugoslavia. Bulgaria too has been fertile country for narrow gauge steam, but the diesels are taking over from the big tank engines. A word of warning here — particularly if there are language problems — the authorities are not really attuned to foreigners taking railway pictures and there can be difficulties. A recent party of enthusiasts was chased by the whole train crew and station staff at a particular narrow gauge terminus and had all their film confiscated, so take care — permission *can* be obtained for responsible groups and it's better that way.

So it will not be long before steam on the narrow gauge, as a common carrier, will be gone in Europe too. But even so there will be a great deal to see for some lines will survive for a while yet with railcars, and the views from them, such as the Nice-Digne in France, are magnificent. It is the scenery and the advent of the enemy in the form of the motor car which have proved to be the saviours of some sections of the narrow

gauge in Europe. Tourists are continually on the move, seeking new outlets and sentiment for steam is still there: both put together have produced viable holiday lines in several countries, Norway, Sweden, Denmark, France, Switzerland and Germany in particular.

The fact that Britain, or rather Wales, was almost certainly the father of this pioneering spirit of preservation sometimes becomes a trifle wearying to those who feel that, once sired, children should be left on their own, and anyway gratitude is a decadent word — even so the relationship continues. Only in March 1970 the *Talyllyn News* which is the magazine of the Talyllyn Railway Preservation Society carried this letter from Monsieur J. Arrivetz:

"As President of the Chemin de Fer Touristique de Meyzieu narrow gauge preservation society and working company, I must point out a fact which will, I am sure, interest the Talyllyn and Festiniog Railway Societies. In the summer of 1968, I went for journeys on the TR and FR. I was already President of the little Meyzieu line, near Lyons, a 1½ mile long undertaking of 60cm gauge, with seven steam locomotives and two diesels. I was most impressed with the Welsh narrow gauge and, back in France, I thought it might be possible to do better than before and gave my CFTM Council a detailed report about your wonderful concerns.

"Three months later, the well-known Vivarais network, 50 miles south of Lyons, was closed by the Government because of a serious money shortage. Soon, we asked about preserving and reopening a part of it, from Tournon (Rhone Valley) to Lamastre (Ardèche). It was very difficult, and no one in authority thought it would be possible to work such a rural line purely as a tourist carrier. We argued for eight months, and one of our best arguments was to show photographs of crowds queuing for, and boarding the trains, at Towyn and at Portmadoc, and these made the local authorities sit up and think. Eventually, we received authority to work the line from June 15th, 1969.

"Then days after, our first steam train climbed along the line. In four months, without any advertising (it was too late for this to be effective), we carried 12,000 passengers. We now run a winter service, with diesel railcars, and already 1970 looks like being 'passenger expansion year'. Our Chemin de Fer du Vivarais is 33km (20 miles) long, through difficult country, in a landscape quite similar to the Welsh mountains. The line has four big viaducts, two tunnels, and six stations. The gauge is one metre. We have two Mallet steam locomotives, 0-6-0 + 0-6-0, and expect at least another three from other lines; two diesel locomotives; four railcars; seven passenger coaches (more on the way); and some 60 wagons.

"I must, however, acknowledge that, without the success of the Talyllyn and Festiniog Railways, our project would have failed. Indirectly, your good work has preserved for posterity the most wonderful of the French light railways, and I am delighted to acknowledge it. To pay tribute of recognition and gratitude, you may advise your members that in 1970, every member of the Festiniog Railway Society, will, on showing his or her membership card, be granted children's fares on the Vivarais line, of seven francs instead of ten for a return trip in a diesel train, or ten francs instead of fifteen for a return trip in a steam train.

"The trip on the Vivarais takes half a day. Trains leave Tournon on Saturdays and Sundays (and possibly on Thursdays) at 10·00 and 14·40, with extras as the traffic demands. We would be delighted to see you."

Europe therefore is well worth a visit — but just think what it was like twenty-five years ago!

FRANCE

Above: Steam has now gone for good from the St Valery-sur-Somme and Noyelles branches of the metre gauge system still operated by the Société Générale Des Chemins de Fer Economiques out of Cayeux in Normandy, but at least trains still run. Back in 1955 the little 2-6-0 tanks were working hard—here in August of that year is No 3851 leaving St Valery (Canal) with the 16.59 train from Noyelles.

Above right: Still in the land of the living is the Le Blanc-Argent line but steam has gone long since. No 21 rusts away at the terminus. This is one of the lines actually owned by the SNCF but operated on its behalf by a private company. Its history was chronicled as long ago as 1955 by M. Gauthier, a local schoolmaster, under the fitting title of *Les 50 Ans d'un Tortillard.*

Right: The finest system of them all was the Reseau Breton whose geographical and engineering centre was at Carhaix in Finisterre. From here some 237 miles of metre gauge track radiated through Brittany, and forty passenger trains a day set off over the system's five main lines. Here, within half an hour, Carhaix's long island platform has seen the departure of trains to connections with Morlaix and Guingamp in the north, Loudeac in the east, and Chateaulin in the west; the railcar in the foreground is about to set off over the fifth RB branch, that to Rosporden on the Lorient to Quimper main line.

Far right: One of the Reseau Breton's 0-6-6-0 Mallet tanks takes a freight over the Guingamp line out of Carhaix. This is the only section on the original narrow gauge system still open but it has been converted to standard gauge.

Tulle is the terminus of a branch running from Brive on the SNCF main line from Paris to Toulouse. Here one could find until comparatively recently two separate metre gauge railways, both operated by SCETA the 'odd jobs' division of the SNCF. The first to go was the Tramway de la Correze running to Neuvic d'Ussel but the former Paris Orleans Correze system to Argentat in one direction and Uzerche in the other remained open until the end of 1969 — the last regular narrow gauge line in France to have an operating (rarely) steam engine in an 0-4-4-0 Mallet Tank. The photograph (*top*) shows a Tramway de la Correze train arriving at Tulle main line terminus. A view (*above*) of the loco shed at Tulle shows engines from the PO Correze line.

Right: Sadly, the whole length of the Reseau du Vivarais, (once a Departmental system) is no more, but fortunately two lengths of it have been saved for posterity. A section of the line from Tournon to Lamestre has been retained by a private company as a 'Chemin der Fer Touristique', using rail cars and occasionally one of the 0-6-6-0 Mallet tanks. The northern section from Dunières to St Agrève is also enthusiast-run. Here is one of the Swiss built engines on a short freight at St Martin in 1960.

30

There is one remaining large narrow gauge system in France. This extends inland from Nice climbing over 3,000ft into the Alpes Maritimes alongside the Route Nationale to Digne where it shares a station with the SNCF. It is a scenic line par excellence and a journey over its metals can be thoroughly recommended. There is no steam now out of Nice but here (*below*) are some of the locomotives which once stormed up into the hills, waiting forlornly for the breaker's torch. The photograph (*bottom*) shows the grand terminus at Nice of the narrow gauge railway to Digne showing the date 1892.

Right: France also sported a number of small railways which were really sugar beet lines and functional only during the winter's harvesting season. One of these was the Reseau de la Sucrerie de Maizy, not far from Reims. In this photograph No 2 (an 0-6-0 tank built by Hainault SA Couillet and their No 1586 of 1910) starts away from Baslieux with a heavy train in October 1963.

LUXEMBOURG

French built buses now run over the streets which once heard the friendly clang of the electric tram and the shrill whistle of the steam engines which hauled the trains out to Echternach, but in the first decade after the close of World War II both electricity and steam could often be seen side by side. Eric Russell's picture of the tram was taken running up the Avenue de la Liberté just beyond the Central Station. It was used to precede the 7.55am Echternach steam train to change the electrically operated points along the city streets.

Inset right: Chemin de Fer Luxembourg owned these lovely 0-4-4-0 Mallet tanks which often headed the Echternach trains.

HOLLAND

No narrow gauge railways as such now operate in Holland, the last to go being the Rotterdam Steam Tram which worked its services with railcars and trailers hauled by diesel locomotives for its last years. The steam tram 0-4-0s, complete with skirts, came out on high days and holidays but their appearances, apart from shunting duties at Rotterdam, were rare. The photograph (*right*) shows a train of modern stock at the terminus at Oostvoorne and (*below*) steam tram engine No 54 at Rotterdam.

Below right: The Geldershe tram made its final journey on August 31st, 1957. It ran from Doesburg to Doetinchem and the engine shown in the photograph, *Silvode*, named after a small village near the German border, has been preserved.

SWITZERLAND

Far left: The only regularly operated steam line in Switzerland today is the Rothorn Bahn running out of Brienz. On the day that this picture was taken a school special formed the first train of the morning. It ran in three parts with the result that the return service was also run in triplicate. Here are two of these trains on the journey back home, taken from the coach of the first.

Left: Several of Switzerland's narrow gauge lines operate the odd steam engine on special occasions and the Furka Oberalp Bahn was one of these for many years. This picture shows No F.O.4 with train No 308 from Brigue to Oberwald on the second rack section just below Fiesch.

Below left: The state-owned narrow gauge line from Interlaken to Lucerne kept two of its steam locomotives in reserve until very recently, using them for emergencies, and sometimes lending them in high season to the Bernese Oberland Bahn as bankers. Here is an enthusiast-chartered special behind 0-6-0 rack tank No 1068 leaving Meiringen.

Below: Switzerland, like other countries in Europe, operated a number of short industrial railways. This line operated by Renfer at Biel-Mett was just 1km long and was used to transport standard gauge wagons between the main line and the factory. The engine is SLM 2095 of 1910 and once belonged to the Lausanne-Echallens-Bercher railway; she was photographed in March 1962.

ITALY

Above: The Bari-Barletta steam tramway in south-eastern Italy did not long survive the war, but it really was a magnificent line. Its engines, in our day, were generally the line's original 0-6-2 tanks built by the Society St Leonard of Liège in 1881 — the rolling stock usually four-wheelers with longitudinal wooden seats. Here is a typical train at Ruvo behind No 9.

Right: Probably the best known of Italy's narrow gauge lines was that which ran from Chiusa to Plan in the Dolomites, known as the Val Gardena railway. Its trains ran summer and winter, and in the high seasons of both, they were crowded with tourists and skiers. Trackwork and locomotives were maintained to extremely high standards, but it was an anachronism and had to go. The photograph shows a winter's train near Selva.

Below: Another narrow gauge line still runs out of Bari the MCL (Mediterraneano-Calabro-Lucane). This system also spread over the heel and toe of Italy, comprising nine geographically isolated lines totalling over 400 miles, all situated in more or less difficult country. The gauge is 95cm. One of the rack sections climbs up for just over 1¼ miles at 1 in 10 on the line from Catanzaro (FS) station to the lofty city station. In September 1959, 2-6-2 rack-and-adhesion tank No 506 stands on the Catanzaro City Shed.

Below right: A further shed scene — this time at Castrovillari with Borsig built 0-8-0 tank No 353.

353

AUSTRIA

Below: Another picture on the Zillertal line, this time of a passenger train leaving Zell for Jenbach in September 1960 behind one of the usual 0-6-2 tanks.

Right: The Zillertal Railway is one of the still independent 76cm lines in Austria. It was opened in stages between 1900 and 1902, and always had an important tourist as well as goods traffic. Although now mostly diesel worked, steam is still alive for tourist traffic and the management is sympathetic to railway enthusiasts. Here is a mixed train in the valley of the river Ziller. The picture shows a train to Mayrhofen behind 0-6-2 tank No 3 in 1956.

Right: The Ybbstalbahn is now a diesel line serving Keinberg-Gaming-Lunz-am-see-Waidhofen and Ybbsitz. It was one of the first of Austria's narrow gauge lines to use the internal combustion engine, though until the mid 1960s these stove pipe chimneyed 0-6-2 tanks could still be seen lined up at the shed at Waidhofen, and occasionally they made a foray into the mountains at the head of a train.

Far right: Here is a picture on the Austrian State Railway of their last completely steam operated narrow gauge line, between Garsten and Klaus, which shows 0-6-2 tank No 298.53 arriving at Grunberg with the 10.58 train from Garsten. This picture was taken in September 1969.

Below: Steiermärkische Landesbahnen: Murtalbahn. To celebrate the 75th anniversary of the opening of this line, now normally dieselised, the 12.30 train from Mauterndorf to Marau-Stolzalpe was worked on Wednesdays, during July and August 1969, by one of these attractive bonneted 0-6-2 steam engines. The train is shown here waiting at Mauterndorf to start the last run of the season. On its return journey it carried a buffet car and the Tamsweg four-piece band.

Below right: The metre gauge Achenseebahn is an astonishing survival. Here, its 0-4-0 rack-and-adhesion locomotive No 2 arrives at the Achensee. The train is pushed by the locomotive up the rack section from Jenbach to Eben and then hauled down a relatively easy, and rackless, descent from there to the terminus at the lake, a most unusual practice. The picture was taken on July 11th, 1956, just as the morning mist was dispersing.

Above left: Giesl Ejector fitted 0-6-2 tank No 699.101 with a passenger train at Eisenkappel in Southern Carinthia. Most of this line is now closed and passenger traffic has gone completely, except for a few steam-operated tourist specials from Weiz to Birkfeld.

Above: On September 30th, 1957 one of Austria's best known and most charming narrow gauge lines closed down for ever. This was the Salzkammergut Lokalbahn which ran from Salzburg to Bad Ischl. Its train was known to the locals as 'fiery Elias', and this picture, double-headed, was taken during the last week of service at Weibenbach.

Far left: Austria's steam-operated rack railway up to Hochschneeberg is run by the state. It starts at Puchberg at the end of an OBB branch line. This train was photographed shortly after leaving the terminus.

Left: The Lanckoronskysche Waldbahn was a 60cm gauge forestry line which closed in the spring of 1958. The railway ran from Steinhaus (where this picture was taken) to Fröschnitz and then into the forest via two rope-worked inclines. Locos Nos 1 and 2 are shown on the train, both being two cylinder 0-6-0 tanks.

Below: This is the Chiem See Railway in Bavaria, a metre gauge steam train which has never owned more than this one locomotive. It is only 2km long connecting the railway station of Prien with the Chiem See port of Stock. It was opened in 1887 and normally only operates in the summer season. The company also owns some ancient paddle steamers on the lake and some motor vessels.

Left: Here is the Chiem See Bahn and its one locomotive again, this time on arrival at Prien from Stock.

Above left: A scene from the former Gernrode-Herzgeroder Eisenbahn in East Germany. This metre gauge line was opened in 1887 and, although a little curtailed just after the war, it is very much as it always has been. The original locomotives, except for one, were removed by the Russians and today the line is run by Mallets from the neighbouring Nordhausen-Wernigerode Railway with which it formerly connected.

Above: A few articulated engines are still working on narrow gauge lines in East Germany. This is a Meyer 0-4-4-0T on the 75cm gauge at Mulda.

Far left: A train on one of the few surviving (but not dieselised) metre gauge lines in West Germany, from Mosbach to Mudau. This line was originally owned by the state of Baden.

Left: In pre-war Germany several extensive 60cm networks were in operation. After the war, one of the few remaining was the Mecklenburg-Pommersche Kreisbahn in Eastern Germany. It was opened from 1892 onwards: the last section of the system, the Friedland-Anklam line, closed only in 1969. The picture here shows a passenger train behind 0-8-0 No 99.3462, built as recently as 1934.

Above: The Brohltalbahn is one of the last narrow gauge railways reaching the Rhine. It was opened in 1901/1902 and runs west from the river at Brohl for about 24km. It is now run by diesels and for goods only, but until recent years a passenger service was operated with some old non-standard railcars and a very attractive trip it was. Part of the line was formerly rack-operated but after the arrival of some heavier engines, among them some Mallets, (one of which is shown here) the rack sections were discontinued.

Above right: The Plettenburger tramway was a friendly line and these enclosed Henschel locomotives operated the service. It was always a little difficult for the enthusiast to identify these engines by their numbers as the company adopted a similar system to that used by the British LNWR in giving new engines the numbers of scrapped or sold ones. Until the late 1950s the railway operated a passenger service to Weisenthal though this picture shows a 'private siding' branch.

Right: The Forster Stadteisenbahn metre gauge line was one of the very few private railways in East Germany which was not taken over by the state. It was opened in 1893 and filled the town of Forst with metre gauge tracks connecting all important industries with the standard gauge station. There was no passenger traffic, but standard gauge goods wagons were conveyed by means of *Rollböcke,* as here. There were eight metre gauge locomotives and two for standard gauge. The line survived until about eight years ago. One of the locomotives is preserved in Dresden. The picture shows a manoeuvre going on in mid-street.

99 3312
K 44₃
Deutsche Reichsbahn

BIERVERLAG
HANS NIELSEN
LBSCHLOSS BIER
10

Above left: This is an engine of one of the only two 60cm systems operated by the State Railways of East Germany. The extensive network was centred on the little spa of Müskäu on the German-Polish border. There has never been any passenger traffic; much of the freight came from the glass industry in the neighbourhood. The locomotive is 0-8-0 No 99 3312

Above: The Port of Emden is the mainline railhead for the island of Borkum. The gauge here was 90cm and the traffic during the fifties was such that the section between Borkum-Reede and Borkum-Stadt was double tracked. Here is the engine shed with the island's two steam locomotives.

Far left: The narrow gauge line which ran along the length of the island of Sylt off the Friesian coast was long an attraction for visitors and photographers. Here is a train at Westerland in steam days (1956) behind an 0-4-2 tank engine.

Left: Along the north side of the Rhine opposite Bonn, the Königswinter rack railway ran to the Drachenfels. Here is a train at the start of the gradient.

FINLAND

Above: This is a winter scene on the 75cm gauge Loviisa-Wesijärvi Railway, opened in 1900 and taken over by the State Railways during the 1950s: they rebuilt it to the standard Finnish gauge of 5ft. The picture shows an Orenstein & Koppel 2-6-0 taking water at a well protected tank.

Above right: From Hyvinkää, about 25 miles north of Helsinki, a 75cm line 28 miles long (opened in 1911) ran to Karkkila. It lost its passenger service in 1961 and closed about 1965. The picture shows 2-8-2 tank engine No 4 in the good Finnish winter in March 1957, at the Hyvinkää (wood) fuelling stage.

Below: Here is another train on the Hyvinkää-Karkkila Railway. The locomotive is 2-8-2 tank No 5 and the train is the 6am mixed to Karkkila. The picture was taken in 1960.

Right: The third Finnish narrow gauge line was the Jokioisten Rautatie which ran from Humppila (on the Turku-Tampere line) to Forssa. This was also 75cm gauge but it had some modern locomotives, Belgian 2-6-2 outside-frame tank engines built as recently as 1947. Here is one of them at Forssa.

SWEDEN

Left: Sweden had two gauges below standard, 3ft 6in, mostly in the south, and the odd gauge of 2ft 11in or 89.1cm. At one spot at Växjö there was a small stretch of four-rail track. Various combinations were seen at different times and here we have a picture of a standard gauge 2-6-2 tank engine shunting standard gauge wagons on to 89.1cm gauge carrier trucks.

Below left: Here is an attractive old tank engine with Swedish pattern spark-arresting chimney. She is 0-6-0 tank No 8 on the 89.1cm gauge at Langshyttan on the Byvalla-Langshyttan Järnbane. The photograph was taken in 1960.

Below: Another picture on the Byvalla-Langshyttan line. Here we have 2-8-0 No 5 *Thor,* built in 1909, at Stjärnsund, on the 89.1cm gauge.

Right: This picture shows Mallet 0-6-6-0 No 12 of the Dala-Ockelbo-Norrsundet Railway, one of the last private 89.1cm lines in Sweden. The tracks have now been torn up but, although it was without passenger traffic for many years, the line carried considerable freight until its owners, a paper mill, changed to road transport in 1967. The line ran through attractive wooded country about 150 miles north of Stockholm. No 12 was built by Atlas of Stockholm in 1910.

Below: Still on the Dala-Ockelbo-Norrsundet line and we have a close-up of Mallet 0-6-6-0 No 8 at the shed. It is not clear what is happening to the chimney.

Below right: The 89.1cm gauge Stockholm-Roslagen Railway ran as an independent line out from the north of Stockholm for many years before being absorbed by the State Railways, the SJ. The picture here shows the junction at Rimbo. Much of the line in the Stockholm suburbs is electrified but steam still survived on the outer lines until about twelve years ago. The picture shows 2-6-2 tank engines Nos 19 and 22.

OCKELBO

NORWAY

Inset: The south of Norway had two narrow gauge lines which operated as common carriers until recent years. One of these was the 75cm gauge Aurskog-Höland line which ran through some very attractive country to the east of Oslo near the Swedish border. Part of the line is preserved as a tourist attraction in the summer thanks to some local enthusiasts. The picture shows 2-6-2 locomotive *Björkelangen* on the turntable.

Left: The other line in the south of Norway, the Byglandsfjord Railway, was 3ft 6in gauge, the last remains of a narrow gauge network which ran at large across the country. The Byglandsfjord line ran through very beautiful country in from the coast to the south-west of Oslo. A few miles have been kept alive by enthusiasts for tourist traffic and trains run in the summer.

DENMARK

There are two pictures here
showing locomotives of the
Görlev sugar factory in Denmark
which ran until the early sixties,
carrying sugar beet in western
Zealand. Steam haulage was
common on these sugar railways
until about ten years ago, with a
variety of locomotives. Here we
have some Jung tank engines
well turned out in green.

POLAND

Far left: This photograph was taken at Bialosliwie, formerly Weiseenhöhe, on an extensive network of 60cm lines. These were private railways until 1945. Originally opened by the Germans, they became Polish, then during the war again German and finally Polish. The network consists of the former Wirsitzen Kreisbahn, with headquarters at Bydgoszcz (or Bromberg). It is serving an agricultural area, and certainly looks as it did 40 years ago. The rolling stock is modernised and in good condition.

Below: Px class 0-8-0 No 48.1784 on the Polish 75cm gauge at Patnow.

Left: This photograph was taken on the Stargard-Dobra-Nowogardzkie line of the Polish Railways. This is a metre gauge road and until 1945 was part of the German Saatzigerkleinbahnen, a 120km system opened from 1895 onwards. The area which this line operates became part of Poland after World War II. The locomotive here is taking water from a stand pipe at the side of the line.

Below left: Here is a train on a 75cm gauge line of the Polish State Railway at Otwock near Warsaw. The locomotive is 0-6-2 tank Ty 2.28.41.

HUNGARY

MAV No 490.222 approaches a road crossing near Miskólc with a miners train in June 1962. This line is 76cm gauge.

YUGOSLAVIA

There are still many miles of narrow gauge in Yugoslavia and one of the least known sections, now freight only and not long for this world, is the metre gauge line up in the north in the area around Osijek in Slavonia. Here is a nice mixed train behind 0-6-2 tank engine No 43 *Zagreb* at Valpovo. The stock and engines of this line were considerably smaller than those running on some narrower gauges.

ZAGREB
43

Above: The greater part of the narrow gauge mileage in Yugoslavia is 76cm or 2ft 6in and a large number of steam locomotives of all types, including-rack-and-adhesion, were built for these lines. The most numerous class, over 100 in all, were the 0-8-2 tender engines with a huge bonnet to arrest sparks capping their chimneys. Here is a mixed train behind one of these at Bresnila on the Sarajevo-Dubrovnik line, now partly replaced by a new standard gauge railway.

Right: Standard and narrow gauge meet at Lasva, near Sarajevo: an 11 class 4-8-0 passing a Class 83 0-8-2.

Below: The last track section in Yugoslavia was between Travnik and Donji Vakuf, on the Lasva-Jajce line. A 97 class 0-6-4T prepares to bank a train out of Travnik.

Below right: A 73 class 2-6-2 on a mixed train for Jajce at Lasva.

73·018

Left: The 60cm line in Macedonia running from Gostivar to Lake Ohrid was a must for all railway enthusiasts who could get to this obscure point. The locomotives were German military 0-8-0Ts of World War I and the coaches and goods stock were primitive in the extreme. These little tanks could only handle the most trivial loads, and the line was mountainous, scenic and decrepit.

Above: Here is BBC Producer Bob Symes-Schutjmann and one of our authors waiting at a counter in a narrow gauge dining car on the 76cm section of the Yugoslav Railways between Dubrovnik and Sarajevo. 2ft 6in gauge diners are not common and on this line eating and drinking was certainly not comfortable with incessant tunnels and curves.

Below left: A rare bird is a JZ 0-10-0 tank No 1362 with a passenger train on the now abandoned Olovo to Han Pijesak section of the narrow gauge.

Below: Another peculiar engine — this is an 0-10-0 tank based on the Lultermöller system when the leading and training axles are coupled by tooth wheels. There were only two of these locomotives of this Class 89 or the JZ and they were used as bankers to the heavy copper ore trains on the Metounica to Bor line, now standard gauge.

Bulgaria has some splendid 2-10-2 tank engines on the 76cm gauge and here is a double-headed train from Septemvri to Dobrinishle behind 615 and 605 near Cepina. This line is now dieselised, but some of these engines survive in the north of the country at Cervenbreg.

Right: Here is another photograph of one of the massive 2-10-2 tanks of the Bulgarian narrow gauge, No 613 at Septemvri. These locomotives were Polish-built.

BULGARIA

ROMANIA

Pictures of the Romanian narrow gauge are a rare find and we have not succeeded in discovering any before. However, two of our indefatigable travellers have come up to scratch as so often in the past and provided excellent pictures for us. The one (*below*) shows 0-6-2 tank No 395005 on the 76cm gauge line from Alba Julia to Zlatna at a wayside halt. The picture (*right*) shows a passenger train in the main street of the town of Agnita. This line was built when this part of Romania belonged to Hungary and the 0-6-0 tank bears its old Hungarian number 388.002. This section through the town has now been abandoned and a new station constructed on the outskirts. It has been said that this whole line will be converted to the standard gauge in due time.

GREECE

Above left: The Peloponnesian Railway in Greece, known as the SPAP until it became part of the state system, was responsible for the extensive metre gauge system south and west from Athens. With a considerable traffic between Piraeus, Athens, Corinth and Patras, the line is now largely diesel-hauled but some attractive engines have worked over the system in part years. The picture here shows the German-built 2-8-0 No 727 and 2-6-0 tank engine   No 538 at Corinth in September 1962.

Above: At the end of the war a large number of American-built 2-8-2 engines were shipped all over the world for narrow gauge operation. A number of these 'MacArthurs' found their way to Greece and here is No 7103 in the metre gauge SPAP passenger station at Athens.

Left: Among the attractive locomotives on the Peloponnesian Railways were the little 2-6-0 tank engines Class Z built in Belgium at the beginning of the century for working the branch line trains around the Peloponnesian Peninsula. Here is No 504 with a train from Patras to Kalamai.

Below: Here is a picture of one of the metre gauge Breda 2-8-2s built by the Italians after the War for the SPAP at Patras, with a big freight train passing along the docks. The 2-8-2 is No 7117. The picture was taken in October 1964.

Right: A principal engineering feature of the SPAP in Greece is the crossing of the Corinth Canal. A single line of railway crosses the canal with its steeply sloped sides at a height, we would suppose, of some 100 feet above the water level. The bridge shown here has been rebuilt since the war as both the road and rail bridges and the walls of the canal itself were blasted by the Germans on their departure from Greece in 1944. The engine shown here is a German-built 2-8-0 of prewar vintage.

Far right: Photographs of the Greek railway running in the area of Missolonghi on the north side of the Gulf of Corinth are rare indeed, but here is one which we think is of sufficient interest to print. It shows a derelict 0-6-0 tank No 7003 *Agrinion* in the yard at Missolonghi in 1964. The town's greatest claim to fame is that Byron died there in 1824.

Below/Below right: A sad loss in the last couple of years has been the end of steam traction on the Diakofto-Kalavryta Railway which runs up from the Gulf of Corinth into the hills inland. This was a 75cm line with one section using rack assistance. The five 0-6-2 tank engines were survivors from a bygone age; four of them were built by Cail and the fifth by Krupp. The locomotives were lying derelict in the yard at Diakofto in the summer of 1969 and a diesel railcar had taken their place.

ΜΕΓΑ ΣΠΗΛΑΙΟΝ
MEGA SPILEON
2

Left: The narrow gauge Thessaly lines in central Greece were of two gauges, the metre gauge which ran from Vólos on the Aegean to Kalambaka with a 2ft gauge section from Vólos to Miléai. The photograph shows one of the metre gauge engines, 0-6-0 tank No 1055, formerly a rack-and-adhesion locomotive from the Brünig line. The picture was taken at Vólos in 1961.

Above: The 2ft gauge line from Vólos to Miléai was a great attraction for years, particularly as it ran down the main street of Vólos where, as an added feature, the rails of standard, metre and 2ft gauge were combined in one four-rail section. Here is 2-6-0 No 101 on the mixed train from Miléai.

Below: On the quadruple line track of the Vólos-Miléai line the train for Miléai waits to pass the Vólos train on the outskirts of that town.

Below left: Here are two of the 2-6-0 tanks of the 2ft line from Vólos to Miléai in the yards at Vólos. These little engines were built by Haine St Pierre in 1912 and were named *Melion* and *Iason.*

PORTUGAL

Above: The spick and span finish of the narrow gauge locomotives of Portugal is epitomised in this view of a 2-4-6-0 Mallet with a mixed train on a hot September day. The burnished copper chimney cap and the general air of wellbeing about the locomotive are a delight to the eye.

Right: Six metre gauge lines and systems still survive in northern Portugal, four running north from the Douro Valley, one around Oporto itself and this, the Viseu line, south-east of Oporto. Here is the evening Viseu-Santa Comba Dao train near Figueiro in 1968 headed by Borsig 4-6-0 tank No E121 built in 1908. The charming old Portuguese coaches are always spotlessly kept.

C.P.
E 121

Above: One of the tributary lines out of the Douro Valley runs up to the city of Braganza from which one of the Queens of England came. The picture shows the afternoon mixed train clambering up the hot tributary valley behind 2-6-0 tank No E82. The locomotive is one of a group of Esslingen tanks built in the eighties.

Above right: The Henschel Mallet tank engines of the Portuguese narrow gauge are still in service and beautifully kept. Here is 0-4-4-0 No E169 manoeuvring empty stock at Senhora da Hora station near Oporto. For the lovers of old coaches, the narrow gauge coaching stock of Portugal is as attractive as the steam engines, the paint a deep rich green except for the crimson mail coaches, and some modern coaches in blue and grey.

Right: There is some big modern stock on the Portuguese metre gauge as well as the charming older material. Here is a Henschel 2-8-2T at Senhora da Hora with some modern coaching stock to match its massive appearance. These big engines can really move fast but, for our part, the little copper-capped tanks are more attractive.

SPAIN

Above left: The 2ft gauge Guardiola a Castellar d'en Huch Railway was situated up on the Spanish slopes of the Pyrenees in the north of Cataluña and existed largely for the limestone and cement traffic. Here is an empty train of stone wagons trundling along on a summer's day.

Above: The La Robla Railway is one of the most active metre gauge lines in the north of Spain. It serves as a connecting link of 207 miles between Bilbao and León. For years it maintained a large and active list of steam locomotives, though is now operated by diesels. The picture here shows express Pacific No 184, which was brought over from the Tunisian Railways when these were dieselised in the early 1950s.

Far middle left: A most attractive line down on the Levant coast was the Onda-Castellón 75cm gauge line which ran from the coast and harbour station of Castellón de la Plana up along the side of the main road for two or three miles and then into the town, round the city streets and out into the country. The little green engines were mostly 0-6-2s and here is one of them, No 8 a compound, being turned by the old Armstrong process on the turntable at Castellón shed.

Far bottom left: A little further south and beyond Valencia to the south was the Alcoy-Gandía Railway which is now closed. It was run for years by an attractive family of Beyer Peacock 2-6-2 tank engines painted black with yellow wheels and copper-capped chimneys. One of these—No 1 *Gandia*—is shown on the turntable at Gandía in this picture.

Left: The Santander-Bilbao Railway was a considerable steam line which is now run by diesels. In its stock was a very pretty group of 4-4-0 tank engines built by Dübs. This one is No 103 *Marón* on a train from Valmaseda to Santander, in typical hilly country.

Above: Another recent closure in Spain is the San Feliú—Gerona line which ran on the 75mm gauge. The attractive little 0-6-2 Krauss tank engines were frequently used in pairs and here are a couple of them back-to-back at Llagostera station.

Above right: In the north of Spain the Langreo Railway was an attractive one to visit as it had in mid-section a rope-hauled Inclined Plane. The trains were marshalled at the bottom or the top of the incline and hauled up or down by means of a winding engine driving an endless rope. This section has been superseded by a long curve and tunnel. The Langreo Railway had locomotives from Belgium, Holland and the USA and just before it turned over to diesels it acquired some steam locomotives from Alaska, of all places. The Langreo line ran on a gauge of 4ft 8½in which is narrow for Spain, whose standard is 5ft 6in or six Spanish feet.

Middle right: The metre gauge Economic Railways of Asturias for years maintained a standard of cleanliness and brilliant finish unsurpassed anywhere in the world. Shining lined-out green paint, polished brass and copper and brilliant dark red under-frames and scarlet buffer beams made a sight for sore eyes. Here is Krauss 2-6-2 tank engine No 35 in the hey-day of this splendid period, the early 1960s. What a pity the diesel ever had to come in to replace such magnificence.

Bottom right: Locomotive No 1 is a rarity but locomotive No 0 is surely unique, even apart from the mechanical pecularity of indirect drive. Here is No 0 of the 2ft 6in gauge railways of the Minas de Aller in the area south of Oviedo. This engine was locally built to the design of Nos 1-5 built by Corpet in 1884. Here many little coal lines still survive, on 2ft or 2ft 6in gauge and at one point on the Fábrica de Mieres coal line where three gauges converged there was a section of four-rail track.

Far right: The Sabero mines north of Cistierna had a considerable section on the 2ft gauge which was run by some very pretty little steam engines, three of which, built in Belgium, are seen resting under the trees on a fine spring day waiting for duty. This is a rainy district and we well remember seeing a battery-driven electric engine hauling some wagons out of the mouth of the mine with the driver holding up an umbrella with one hand and driving with the other.

Far left: One of the sturdiest supporters of steam left in Spain is the metre gauge Ponferrada-Vallablino. This line is basically a coal-hauling road and has some powerful tender engines as well as tanks. The picture shows Engerth type 2-6-0 built in Spain as recently as 1959 by Macosa. A powerful, stocky brute of an engine: may it long survive.

Left: As we have said the Onda-Castellón Railway ran for some distance through the town of Castellón and alongside the main road to the port. This was a constant source of pleasure to the inhabitants of the town and visiting tourists. Here is one of the 0-6-2 tank engines which pulled passenger and freight trains alike, on the section running down to the harbour.

Below left: The big mineral railway working from the iron mines of Sierra Menera at Ojos Negros in Central Spain down to the coast at Sagunto is a considerable undertaking and has only recently gone over to diesel traction. At one time there were some British-built Mallets and some Spanish Garratts in this service. Here is one of each at the mid-point station at Teruel. Although this is a big railway, it has never offered any passenger service.

Below: Down at the coast at Sagunto the Sierra Menera at Sagunto terminal had a lot of traffic with the local iron and steel works and shunting around the yards was carried out by a variety of old tank engines. One of these, a 2-6-2 from the Alcoy-Gandiá, is here seen with some limestone in the yards of the steel works.

Bottom: Here, still on the Sierra Menera, is one of the metre gauge Garratts hauling away a big train of iron ore from Teruel bound for the coast at Sagunto.

Nº 11
F.C. ALLEN

Left: The Utrillas metre gauge line south of Zaragoza was always an attractive line, if only that for many years it was out-of-bounds to enthusiasts who were chased off by a zealous guard carrying an ancient rifle. Here are 2-6-0 tank No 1 and Engerth 2-6-0 No 101 shunting on mixed gauge lines at Zaragoza.

Left: The La Robla Railway had over sixty steam engines in the fifties including a lot of tank engines from various makers, some of great age. Here is a local train out of Bilbao, behind Sharp Stewart 2-6-2 tank No 15 *Cervera,* built in 1894.

Below left: For many years, Solvay & Co had a 2ft gauge line running round their Alkali Works at Torrelavega near Santander, in addition to a metre gauge connection with the Cantabric Railways which runs past the works. Every year, for many years, one of the authors of this book used to pay a visit to Torrelavega Works and was allowed to drive one of the 2ft gauge locomotives. This became such a feature of the annual visit that the locomotive was named after him and at the end of its life in 1963 was shipped over to England as a free gift and now has resumed work at Leighton Buzzard after a pause for refreshment in the author's garage at Battle.

Below: In Majorca the cathedral dominates the city of Palma. Underneath the cathedral and in small and decent proportions the railway runs to the harbour, then passing through a tunnel emerges by the station. This line has the unusual Spanish gauge of 3ft and used a number of pleasant steam engines before succumbing to internal combustion.

USA and Canada

The story of American railroads has been told many times and the ramifications of their growth have been explored and exploited by the storyteller, the film maker and the historian. Beyond the United States of America these stories have been mostly related to Transcontinental lines and tales of Casey Jones, but the men who built the railroads which crossed the Great Divide also had occasion to revert to the narrow gauge. To promoters of limited means, narrow gauge construction had almost unlimited allure. Construction costs of 3ft gauge rights of way, trestles, tunnels and the like were about half those of standard operations, and steep gradients, narrow canyons and mountain fastnesses impervious to standard gauge, save at ruinous cost, were easily available to twenty-ton locomotives and coaches only 33ft long. For a period, as elsewhere in the world, the fallacy of narrow gauge thinking got hold of the Americans in the 1870s and it attracted both engineers and bankers alike — nowhere more so than in the Colorado Rockies.

By the time our period begins, however, even in Colorado the Mecca of the narrow gauge railway supporters, the decline had begun in earnest and very few of the lines still open were operating passenger trains. But it was in the southwest of this state that the narrow gauge lore of America abounded and abounds; it is here that the gold, silver, zinc, lead and uranium ores were found in large quantities. The San Juan country had only been inhabited for ten years when the Denver & Rio Grande Railroad entered the area and built on both the north and south sides of the mountains. Branching off from these main lines came the shorter lines to Silverton, Lake City, and Ouray. Then came the other independent roads — the Silverton Railroad, the Rio Grande Southern, the Silverton Northern and others, plus some later branches of the D&RGW. Of all these the two best remembered must be the Silverton branch and the D&RGS whose history has been so ably recorded by Josie Moor Crum.

The last train on the Rio Grande Southern ran in 1951, Dolores, the last operating station, closed on Christmas Eve and the final revenue train on the system was a freight from Durango to Mancos and return on December 27th. But the narrow gauge lines of the Denver & Rio Grande Western have lasted longer; true, the San Juan' passenger train no longer operates between Durango and Alamosa, and the whole of the main line closed in 1968. But in 1971 a new miracle happened in that the state purchased, and then leased out 64 miles of scenic track from Antonito to Charma over the Cumbres Pass and this section is now in regular operation for tourists using the old D&RGW 2-8-2s and cars. The Silverton train lives on — not because the company wanted it to, but because like so many other narrow gauge lines it was discovered by the tourist in the 1950s, but unlike many it has not been allowed to close. Now, Durango is isolated and it is a matter for conjecture how long the trains of yellow bogie

cars will run up the valley of the Animas River twice a day in high summer. These trains carry in the region of 100,000 passengers during the operating season and are so popular that it is almost impossible to get a seat unless it is booked well ahead. It is to be hoped that the Silverton train, in spite of its slightly gimmicky outline, will continue to give pleasure for many years to come, but it operates under American 'full crew' laws and has to be worked with a crew of five — driver, fireman, conductor and two brake-men, which is an expensive business.

Strange as it may seem, there are other narrow gauge lines operating in Colorado but these, like all other similar roads are enthusiast or tourist-operator owned and run. These include the really excellent Colorado Railroad Museum at Golden, near Denver where trains run behind a Baldwin 2-8-0 operate on high days and holidays, and two running railways, the Central City and the Cripple Creek. The former is built to the American standard narrow gauge of 3ft and trains run over the trackbed of the old Colorado and Southern line from Central City to Black Hawk. The Cripple Creek line is a rare bird in that it is 2ft gauge using a Koppel 0-4-4-0 of 1902 vintage.

Apart from forestry lines the other narrow gauge roads were mainly in New England (in Maine) and built to the 2ft gauge, lines like the Sandy River and Rangely Lakes, and the Bridgton and Harrison. Most of them went the way of all flesh during the Great Depression of the 1930s, but survivors can still be found in Massachusetts. Here, at Carver near Cape Cod is the heritage left by Ellis Atwood and Nelson Blount in a 5½ mile line using vintage equipment, called the Edaville Railroad.

And last but not least on our list, is the remnants of a once prosperous heavy traffic coal hauler, the East Broad Top in Pennsylvania — known to some as the 'Narrow Gauge Capital of the East'. Abandoned in 1956 due to lack of demand for coal, the EBT was saved by a scrap dealer and a portion of it re-opened for tourist operations. Unlike other lines operating for similar purposes, its locomotives and stock are all original, and it even has a roundhouse and workshops. The East Broad Top is probably the nearest, in the East of America today, to the real thing of thirty years back.

Canada has never been narrow gauge country for its great trunk routes were thrust westwards by standard gauge lines and their offshoots were logically standard gauge branches, as were those to such cities as Toronto, Ottawa and Hamilton. Such narrow gauge systems as did exist were short and locally independent, usually with an industrial usage such as forestry. But now that Newfoundland has joined the Great Dominion some 550 miles of narrow gauge main line have been added, and have become part of the Canadian National system. All trains these days are diesel-hauled, but there is some magnificent scenery to explore.

CANADA

Far left: The Newfoundland railway system, now dieselised and part of the Canadian National network, is of 3ft 6in gauge. The rear truck of a 4-6-2 steam locomotive gets a final check before departing from Port aux Basques to St John's, Newfoundland, a distance of 547 miles. This was taken during the summer of 1947, a year or so before the introduction of the diesels.

Left: Here is a mixed train on the Placentia branch near Freshwater in Newfoundland. The train ran three times a week from Argentia to St John's, and the photograph shows Pacific No 196 built by Baldwin about 1935.

Below left: The dieselisation of the Newfoundland lines of the Canadian National Railways was brutal and short, the entire procedure taking only a few weeks. Here is a large shipment of CNR hood type diesels being loaded in Montreal docks late in 1956 for service on the 3ft 6in gauge in Newfoundland.

Below: This picture was taken just at the end of World War II. It shows 3ft 6in gauge 4-6-0 No 119 at St John's. Steam is now entirely gone from Newfoundland.

Right: Up in the far north-west the White Pass and Yukon Railway runs through some formidable territory from Skagway in Alaska up over the Great Divide and down to the Canadian side into the Yukon territory. At the summit of the White Pass the heavy snows sweep down all through the winter and the rotary snow ploughs are kept busy. This line is of 3ft gauge.

Below: The rotary WP&Y snow plough on the bridge over Dead Horse Gulch near the top of the White Pass. During the Gold Rush of 1897/1898 thousands of animals and many human beings lost their lives in the ascent of this fierce coastal range. The Trail of '98 went through Dead Horse Gulch and by the side of the Railway there is a monument to the poor beasts which says:

THE DEAD ARE SPEAKING
In memory of us 3,000 pack animals that laid our bones on these awful hills during the Gold Rush of 1897-98. We now thank those listening souls that heard our groans across this stretch of years
WE WAITED BUT NOT IN VAIN

Below right: Canada has never had much mileage of narrow gauge railway but at one time possessed what was said to be the shortest railway in the world, a three-quarters of a mile line in the Muskoka lakes area at South Portage. This line was really a tourist attraction running a service between two lakes with the aid of two 0-4-0 tanks, one of which in summer used to put in a daily appearance. The engines were little mine locomotives from Nova Scotia but they did not survive the 1950s.

Above: We have always regarded Jim Shaughnessy as one of the great artists with the camera working today. He has made a particular study of the Denver and Rio Grande Western narrow gauge lines between Alamosa and Durango and from Durango on up to Silverton. The Alamosa-Durango line has had a very precarious existence in the last few years, depending on politics rather more than what freight was offered, though part of it is now reprieved; on the other hand the Silverton branch has been a most successful tourist attraction. Here is a freight train labouring up the 1 in 25 on the Cumbres Pass near Chama, New Mexico, with two 480 class 2-8-2s.

Right: Full speed ahead: 'Mikado' No 488 of the Rio Grande approaching the limit of 35 miles an hour on the flat land between Antonito and Alamosa before the serious work of the climb to the passes to the west begins.

GREAT BRITAIN
The Vale of Rheidol is British Railways' only steam operated line. 2-6-2 Tank No 9 *Prince of Wales* blasts her way through the rock cutting near to the summit at Devil's Bridge.
/P. B. Whitehouse

Right: During the first year of its 'preservation' the Isle of Man Railway ran trains over all its sections. Two trains, one for Ramsey and one for Peel wait in Douglas station platform. /C. M. Whitehouse

Below: Almost as built the 0-4-4-0 double Fairlie *Earl of Merioneth* (once *Taliesin*) takes a Dduallt bound train out of Porthmadog Harbour station on the Festiniog Railway. /CMW

Below right: Purchased privately from India 0-6-0 tank *Rishra* takes a train of enthusiasts for a weekend trip on the Leighton Buzzard Narrow Gauge Railway. /CMW

RISHRA

EUROPE
Right: Odd man out. Reseau Breton 0-6-6-0 Mallet tank No 41 (ex-PO Correze) waits for her turn of duty at Carhaix. /*PBW*

Below: A Henschel 0-4-4-0 Mallet tank waits at Porto Trindade station on the CP Metre Gauge. /*PBW*

USA
Far right: Mount Washington Cog Railway rack engine No 8 begins the climb out of Base station. /*PBW*

TIP TOP
MT. WASHINGTON
COG RAILWAY
8

SOUTH AMERICA
Left: National Railways of Mexico 2-8-0 No 273 heads a Mexico-Cuautla train at Chalco.

AFRICA
Below left: South African Railways 2ft Gauge Hanomag Garratt No NG 59 on one of the rare narrow gauge passenger trains approaching Loerie. */PBW*

Below: Preserved South African Class 6 3ft 6in gauge locomotive on a pedestal at Kimberley station. */CMW*

Above: Rhodesian Railways 15th class Garratt just out of Bulawayo shops. /*PBW*

Right: East African Railways 60 class Garratt on a mixed train to Arusha. /*PBW*

On the mixed gauge track a few miles north of Antonito, a narrow gauge stock train heads for the main-line connection at Alamosa. The locomotive is 2-8-2 No 488. This is on the section now reopened as a tourist line.

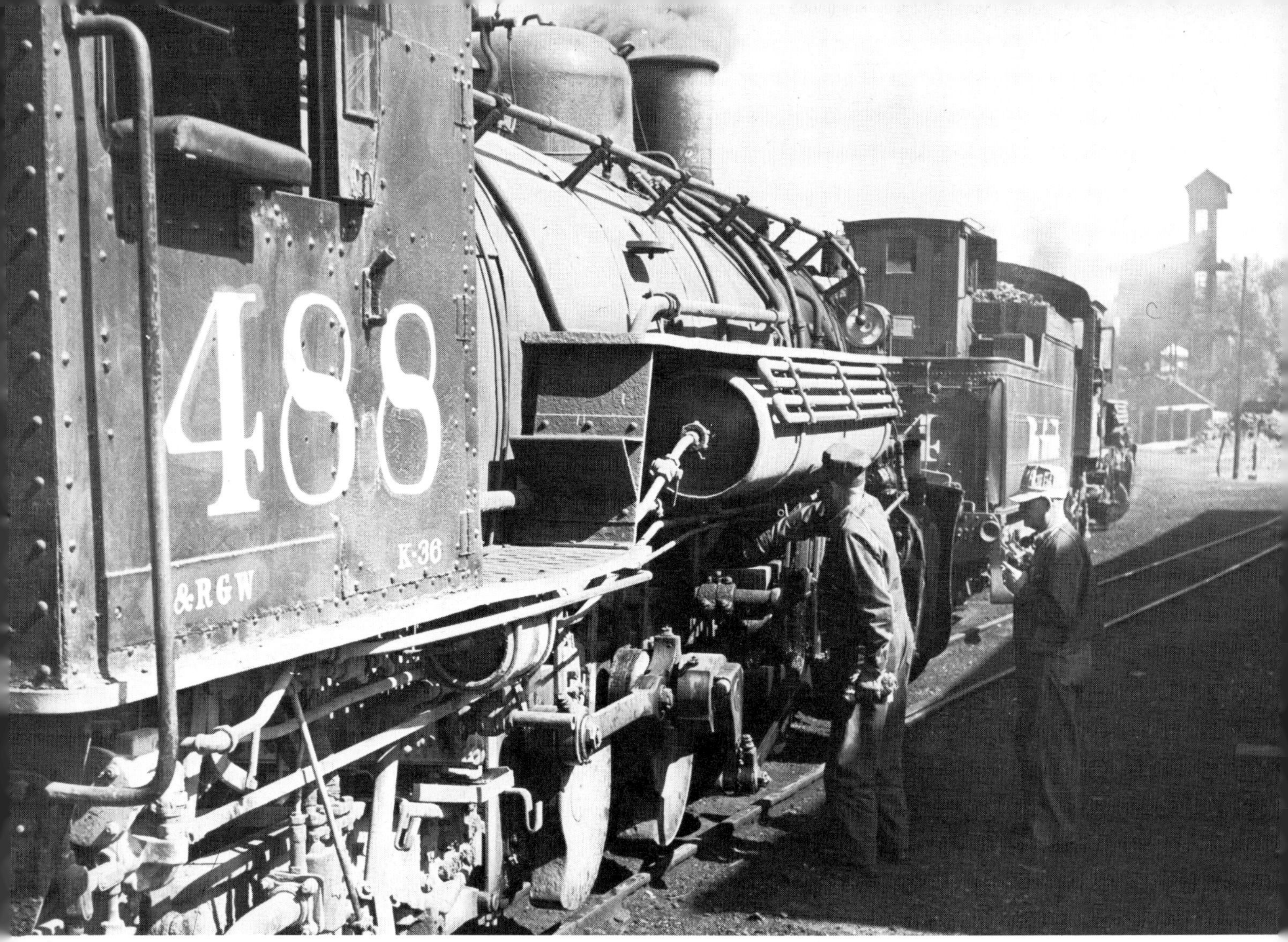
488
K-36
&RGW

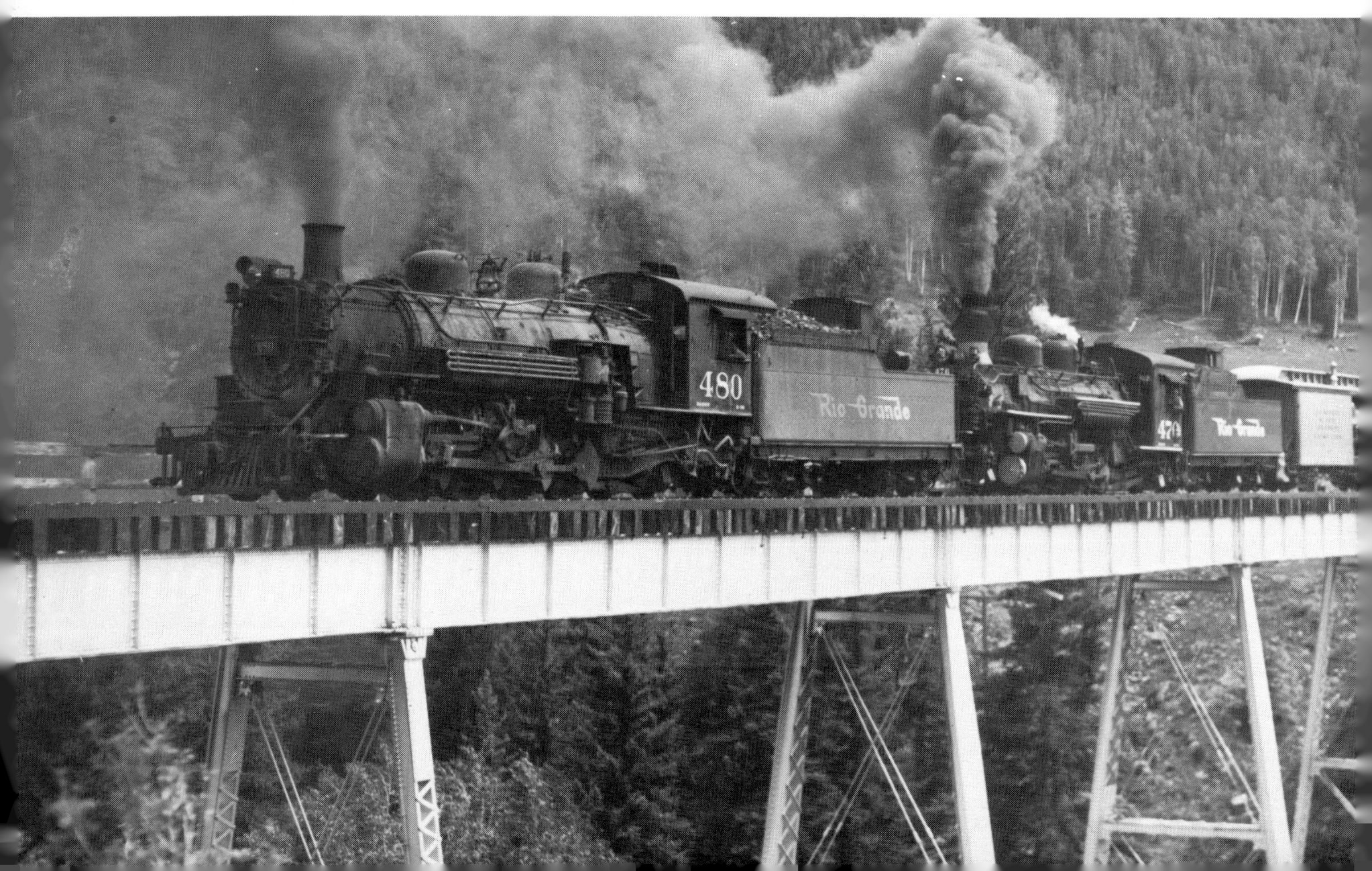
480
Rio Grande

Above left: The engineer of 'Mikado' No 484 looks on at Chama while his mate in charge of 488 adds a last minute drop of oil. In a few moments, both these locomotives will be working freight up the 1 in 25 gradient to the top of the Cumbres Pass, 10,000ft above sea level. Chama is now a terminus of the new Toltec Railway's Tourist Operation.

Above: 484 and 488 preparing for the road at Alamosa, photographed just as the tank of 488 overflows. These 2-8-2s seemingly so small are, in fact, powerful engines with the same sort of tractive force as the 9F 2-10-0s of British Railways. The very similar 490 class were converted from standard gauge locomotives.

Left: A double-headed special passenger train for the Pacific coast chapter of the Railway and Locomotive Historical Society excursion. The locomotives are 2-8-2s, Nos 480 and 476, and the train is starting to climb up to the Cumbres Pass. Railfans can still make this trip over the 64 miles between Chama and Antonito.

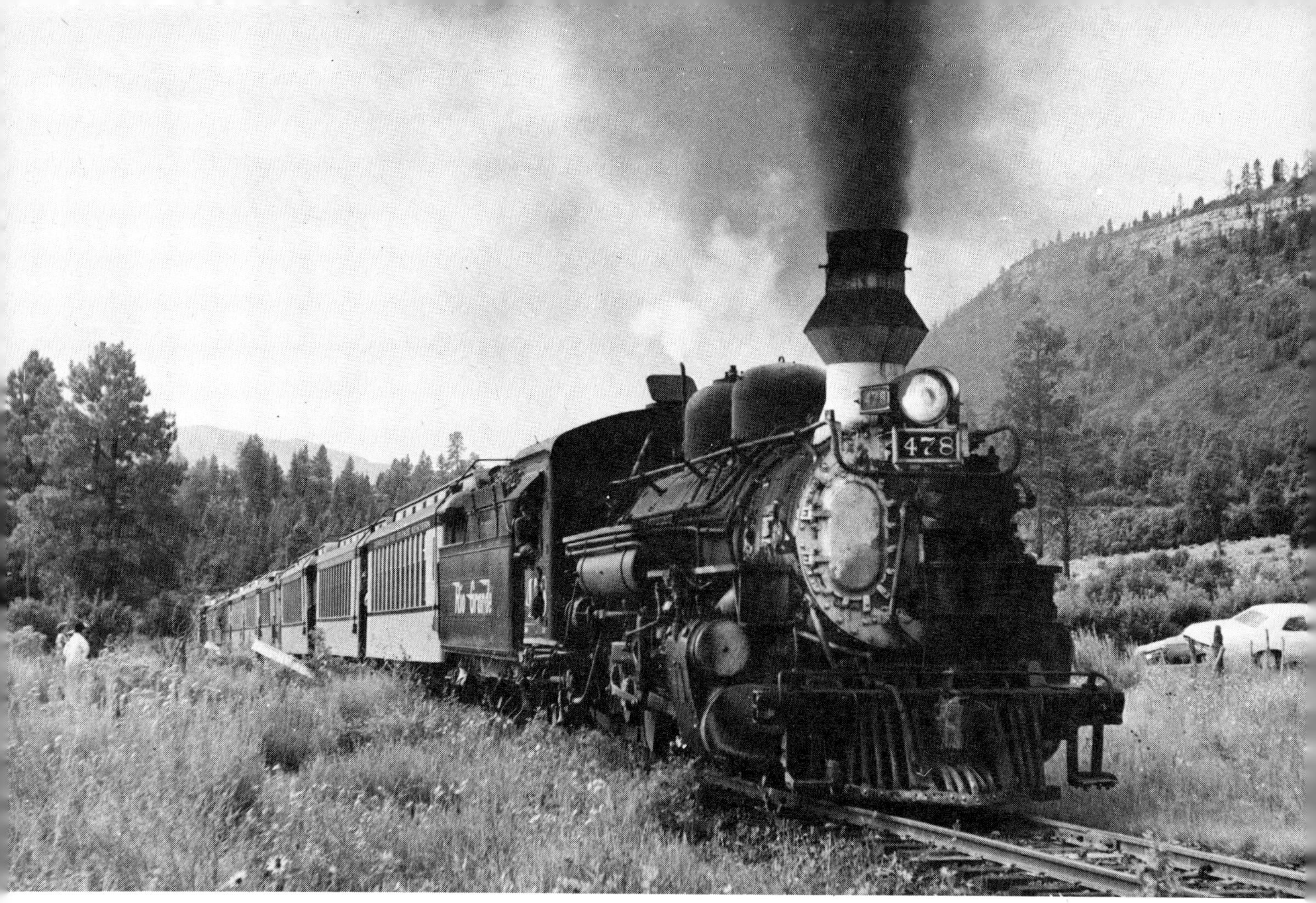
478
Rio Grande

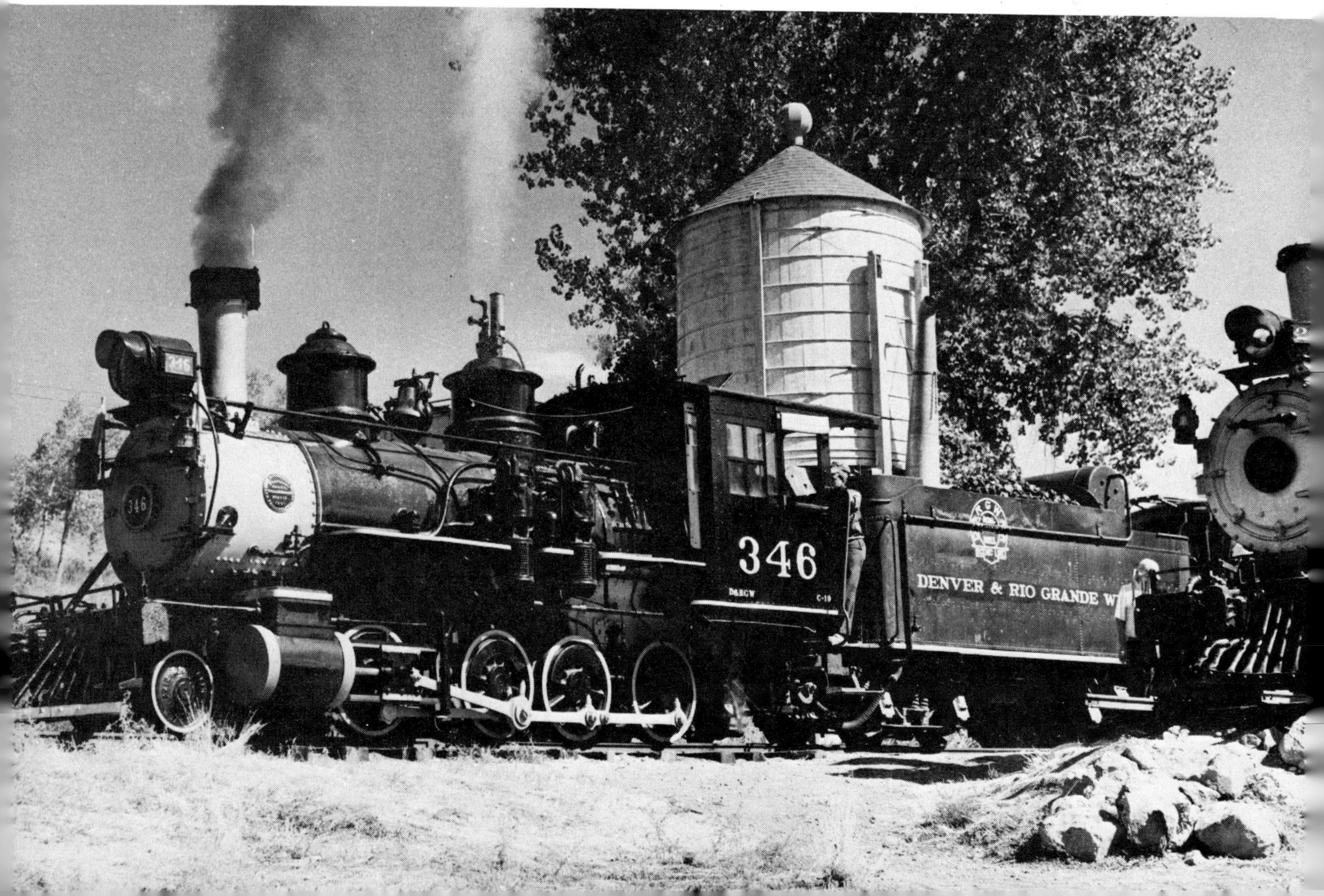
346
D&RGW
C-19
DENVER & RIO GRANDE W

Far left: During the summer of 1969 this Silverton service (which the Company wanted to abandon) carried nearly 100,000 passengers and in the high season ran two trains daily. Here is No 478 near Rockwood.

Left: At Silverton, just at the back of the jail, this relic of the old Silverton Northern RR stands alongside its wooden station.

Below left: The Narrow Gauge Railroad Museum at Golden, Colorado steams its exhibits from time to time. There is even a loco from the nearby Pikes Peak cog railway, now dieselised. Here is a D&RGW consolidation in steam in September 1969.

Below: A 'new' tourist line is being constructed on the trackbed of the old Colorado Central line at Central City and this is well worth a visit. The rear engine is oil burning and comes from Central America.

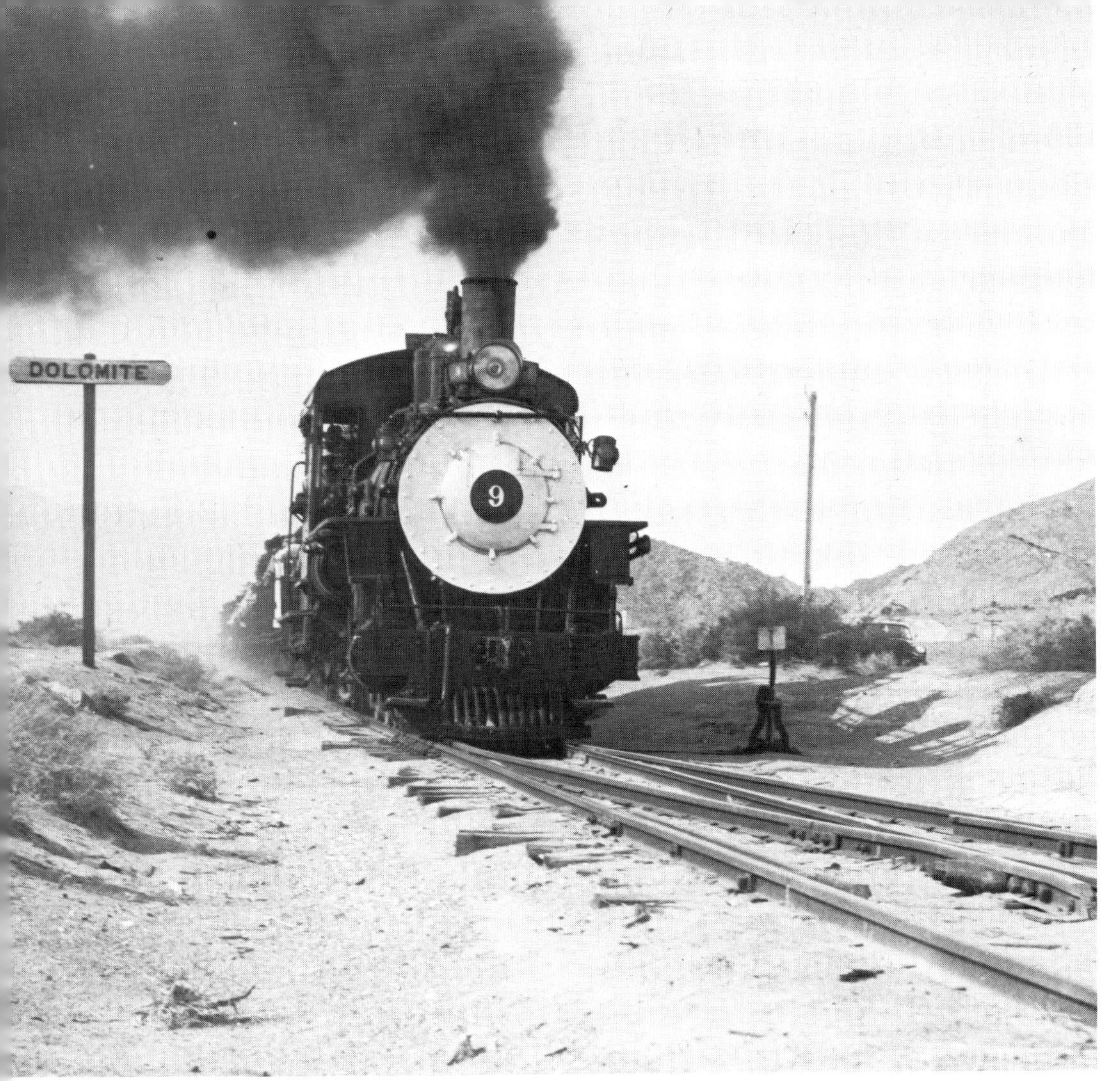
DOLOMITE
9

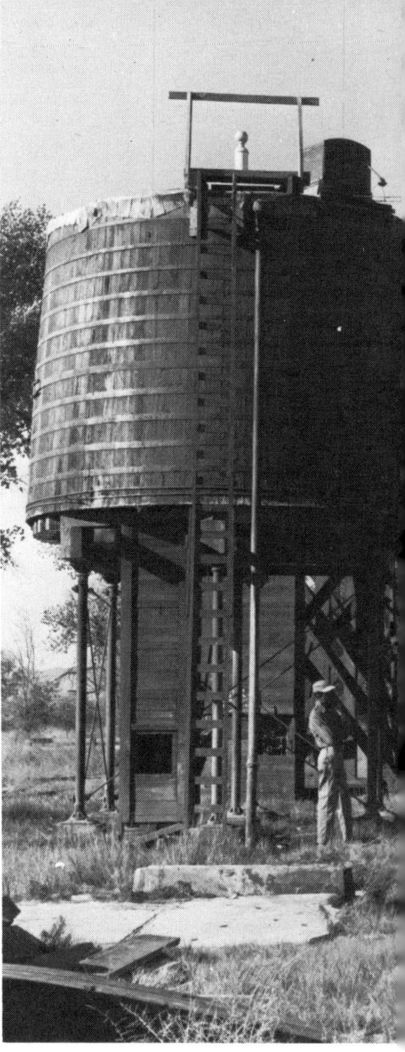

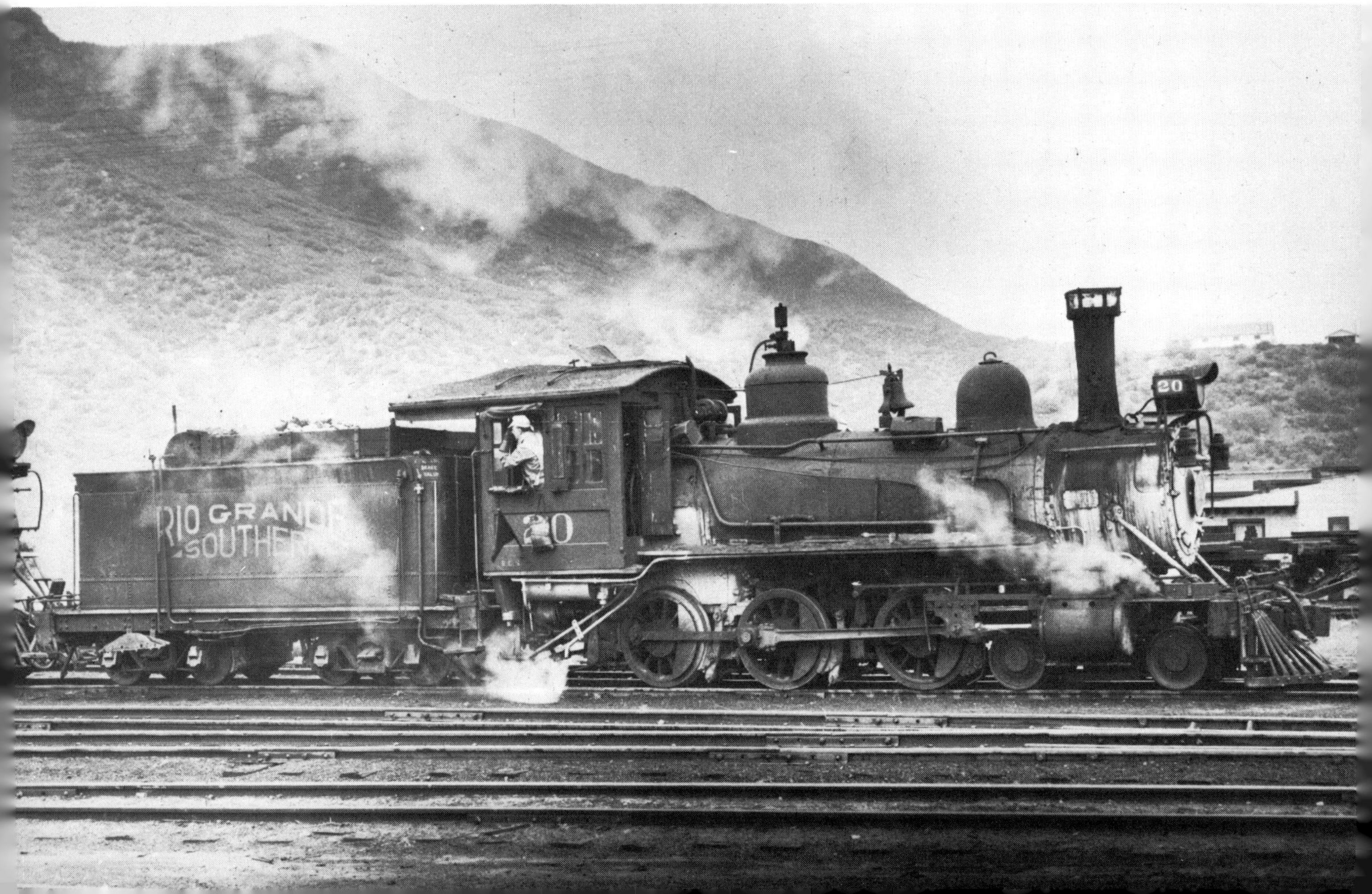
RIO GRANDE
SOUTHER
20
20

A branch of the Southern Pacific Railway survived into the postwar period. This was a 3ft gauge line, the last remnant of the old Carson and Colorado, running from the junction with the standard Southern Pacific line at Owenyo in California southwards to Keeler and northwards to Laws for a total distance of 70 miles. It survived until 1960 with one diesel and one little 4-6-0 with a round tank for a tender. In the last days of the Keeler Laws branch (*far left*), trains occasionally struggled through the desert country behind 4-6-0 No 9. The picture (*left*) might be called 'The end of the line' as it shows the water tower at Owenyo which was then the terminal of the Southern Pacific's Owens Valley branch in 1954.

Below left: As late as 1948 there was vastly more 3ft gauge line in Colorado than survives today, and the independent Rio Grande Southern linked the northern and southern DRGW narrow gauge divisions at Ridgeway and Durango. Here is 4-6-0 No 20 about to take a turn as the pilot of No 74 on a heavy freight bound for Rico. No 20 is the original *Emma Sweeney* of motion picture fame, being used in many epics, including "Ticket to Tomahawk".

Below: Back east in Massachusetts the Edaville Railway, around the cranberry bogs at South Carver, is still going strong. This tourist line uses 2ft gauge rolling stock and locomotives from some of the lines that used to run in the state of Maine. The Edaville line was built on his estate by Ellis D. Atwood shortly after the war. The locomotive here is 2-4-4 No 7, from the Bridgton and Harrison Railroad.

Above: The East Broad Top Railway. This was originally a 3ft gauge coal carrier in the south of Central Pennsylvania. When its activities came to an end in the 1950s, a short length was revived as a tourist attraction making a special feature of runs to attractive picnic grounds. There were some fine 2-8-2 'Mikado' engines on the line and two of them, Nos 12 and 15, are shown here on the turntable at Orbisonia in 1960.

Right: This picture shows an East Broad Top train in its original guise hauling coal near Saltillo, Pennsylvania with 2-8-2 No 17. The picture was taken in March 1956 before the railway changed its activities.

Far right: The East Broad Top Railroad. The 3ft gauge 2-8-2 No 12 *Millie* drops her fire before going on to the turntable, and into the roundhouse for the night, as seen through a roundhouse doorway, with a caboose No 27 at right, at Rockhill Furnace, Pennsylvania.

112

MT. WASHINGTON
COG RAILWAY
SUMMIT

Far top left: East Tennessee & Western North Carolina Railroad. After making connections with the Southern and Clinchfield railways, the ET&W mixed pulled out of Johnson City, Tennessee for Cranberry, North Carolina. 4-6-0 No 8 with heavy freight consist behind the RPO-Coach combine. Note the brakemen riding the tops. This line closed about 1950, but a short section has since been rebuilt as a tourist attraction.

Far middle left: Another view on the East Tennessee and Western North Carolina. This 4-6-0 still works on the tourist operation, which rather regrettably often goes by the unfortunate name of *Tweetsie*, in company with a 2-8-2 from the White Pass and Yukon.

Left: The Argent Lumber Company at Hardeeville, South Carolina had a 3ft gauge railway in swampland, hauling timber to the mills. The locomotives matched the track in age and upkeep but had some of the finest 'cabbage' stacks still in captivity in postwar years. The picture shows 2-6-2 No 5 on the left and 2-6-0 No 2 on the right.

Below left: The Mount Washington Cog Railway, we are glad to say, just qualifies for inclusion in this book as the gauge is officially 4ft 8in. It is very attractive to be able to include it for not only has it got some outlandish locomotives but also it was the first of all the rack railways in the world. Dating from 1869, the track is very steep in places, the severest grade being 37·41 per cent on Jacob's Ladder. The summit of the railway is 6,293ft above sea level. Typical of this attractive line is the fact that it has just constructed a *new* steam locomotive in its own workshops.

Below: The picture is another of Jim Shaughnessy's masterpieces of trains passing on the Cog Railway; two trains are on the ascent and a third is in the siding waiting to go down. The rack ladder is well shown here.

Central and South America

South America is a continent and all the variations of climate and geography which a continent should provide are there — and in full measure. From the volcanic chain of Central America, across the steaming jungles of the Amazon basin — with the Equator crossing the Amazon's mouth — to the high savannahs of Brazil and the flat lands of the Argentine, on down to the chilly windswept plains and mountains of Patagonia and Tierra del Fuego, man is rarely master of his environment and the contrast of manmade development in North and South America is great. This is accentuated by the mountain chain of the Andes pressing close to the western shore, so presenting a formidable barrier to penetration of the hinterland and the wealth of the continent.

So it is not surprising that railway development, except for the great fan of lines radiating from Buenos Aires, is at best a tentative thing and nowhere are to be found the equivalent of the great transcontinental lines of Canada and the USA.

To most of us in Europe, South America remains a dreamland far away, reached only by romantic cruise ships or a refuge for a half-forgotten uncle in desperate flight from the fury of Victorian parents. Here Darwin began to speculate on the Origin of Man; here the great explorer Fawcett was lost for ever in the Matto Grosso, and here his son Brian spent his adventurous railroad career in Chile and Peru — all so vividly and readably set down in his splendid book *Railroads of the Andes*. To read that book is a great joy, but one's mind quickly becomes the fertile recipient of the South American travel bug — at least as an armchair traveller. But indeed in this day and age the former problems of time, distance and finance are not as great as they were, for holidays are longer, air travel quicker, and now we have the development of special holiday tours for enthusiasts which are being offered as packages by several reputable travel agencies including Ian Allan and Thomas Cook. South Africa, East Africa and Australia are already on this list, so why not Central and South America?

Americans, of course, have no such inhibitions for they are used to travelling what to us are immense distances, without a second thought. An example of this is the production of that beautifully illustrated book by our friend Gerald M. Best *Central American Holiday*. This was first published in 1960 and is the story in words and pictures of a tour made by the Pacific Coast Chapter of the Railway and Locomotive Historical Society of America. The tour covered the republics of Salvador, Guatemala and Mexico, where at that time the hoarse voice of the diesel had not yet been heard. In Salvador and Guatemala all the railways are narrow gauge and in Mexico that rare locomotive type today, the 4-4-0, was still to be seen on both the narrow and standard gauge. Today steam is

gone in Mexico but Central America still offers some steam — if you can get there.

In South America the narrow gauge can be found in all countries except Uruguay and there is still much to be discovered. The best-known lines are probably those over the Andes between the Argentine and Chile — the Argentine section runs from Mendoza in the eastern foothills of the mountains for 108 miles to Las Cuevas where the Chilean Railway takes over and carries the train on to the summit at 10,452ft and then for another 44 miles to Los Andes where it meets the broad gauge lines to Santiago and Valparaiso. But these days it is diesel and electric all the way. The railways of the Andes in Peru, the Central and the Southern, are on standard gauge and wonderful railroading they provide but metre gauge runs in from the Chilean coast to the Altiplano of Bolivia and up from Guayaquil to Quito and up from the coast of Colombia on 3ft 6in and 3ft gauge. Steam alas is on the way out on all of these and Colombia is probably the best place for steam in these days.

Brazil is such a huge country that it is hard to know and describe. Over half its railway mileage is metre gauge and the rest on the Irish gauge of 5ft 3in. Electrification in the north and dieselisation all over are reducing the interests of the steam enthusiast and sadly the last five years have seen the loss of the Fell line from Cachoeiras de Macacú and of the Riggenbach rack-line to Petrópolis in the Rio area. Gone too is that raffish Cantareira line of the Sorocabana Railway with its green Baldwin 4-6-0 with copper-capped chimneys.

The metre gauge lines in the Argentine are still numerous threading in amid the 5ft 6in lines especially in the north, and one section of the Argentine system, formerly the Entre Rios Railway, is built on 4ft 8½in, so is technically narrow gauge in Argentina.

In the far south, in Patagonia, it was an enjoyable experience a year or so ago to find a coal hauling railway on 2ft 6in gauge powered by the most modern Japanese steam engines and also to discover on the very shores of the Beagle Channel in Tierra del Fuego, named after Darwin's ship, the relics of the most southerly railway in the world, even if it was laid out to transport convicts.

ARGENTINA

Above: Although a large proportion of the railways of the Argentine, including the international routes to Bolivia and northern Chile, are of metre gauge, there are not many passenger-carrying lines of narrower gauge still in service. That indefatigable researcher, D. Trevor Rowe, however, has found for us the 60cm Ferrocarril Correntino is a tributary of the Urquiza Railway which in turn is Argentina's only 4ft 8½in gauge system. The Correntino line is almost moribund, but a train ran twice a week and here it is at San Luis with 2-6-0 No 681 in August 1968.

Above right: Right down near the lake district of San Carlos de Bariloche in the foothills of the Andes close to the Chilean border is the 75cm gauge system running from Esquel to Ing. Jacobacci. This is another find of Trevor Rowe and he has also provided the photograph of one of the thirty oil-fired 2-8-2s which run the service., The line is part of the General Roca Railway of the Argentine and is a feeder for the broad gauge line running from Buenos Aires to the lakes. The picture was taken at Esquel in January 1969.

Right: Still on the Esquel-Ing. Jacobacci in southern Argentine. Here is a picture of the train in full flight on its way up from Esquel through typical sparse scrubland. Trevor Rowe reports the rolling stock as comfortable and including a restaurant car.

Far right: At the metre gauge Resistencia shed of the Belgrano Railway, we have here Maffei Pacific No 614, photographed in August 1968. She was built in 1911.

Right: Although the metre gauge lines of the Argentine are grouped together under the illustrious name of General Belgrano, they are not all of them connected. Here is a train on the northern section at Tucumán, photographed in 1962 with an American-built 'Mikado' from Baldwin at the head.

Below: The General Belgrano system which has a total mileage of 9,700 has a fine mixed lot of locomotives as its engines came from many sources, such as the old Central Cordoba and the Central Northern before they were merged under one management. Here are a couple of British built Pacifics at the Tapiles shed near Buenos Aires in 1963.

Below right: Another metre gauge scene on the General Belgrano system in the Argentine was provided by this British-built 2-8-2 in the spring sunshine at Rosario. The ultimate origin of these locomotives is uncertain because with fervent but obscure patriotism all reference to the makers was removed.

Right: Still on the General Belgrano metre gauge system, we have here two British-built 2-8-2s, rather similar to the large group of 4-6-2s, bringing a freight train into Tucumán in the hot northland of Argentine. Here is a case — we think not uncommon — where the wagon stock is more modern than the locomotives.

Still in the realm of General Belgrano is a considerable network of metre gauge lines in the south and west of Buenos Aires. These are the 'Provincial' railways of the Buenos Aires district which still offer passenger services. Steam served well into the sixties. The picture (*far top right*) shows a Henschel Pacific No 10,173 at the terminal near Avellaneda, and that (*far middle right*) shows another German engine, this time with a particularly thick chimney, at the same spot. Each has a large oil-carrying tender.

Below: The General Belgrano system included a rack section on the northern line which ran from Jujuy through the eastern fringes of the Andes up to Bolivia. To tackle the 1 in 16 grade with 400 ton trains in tow, two gigantic 0-12-2 rack-and-adhesion engines were built.

Below right: In the far south of the Argentine in Patagonia, just a few miles north of the Straits of Magellan, is the Rio Turbio railway running inland from the Atlantic port of Rio Gallegos into the coal measures in the Andean foothills to the west. This is a surprisingly active and lively line, although running on 2ft 6in gauge. Some recent Japanese locomotives have been supplied and these are very substantial machines with a 2-10-2 wheel arrangement and 12-wheeled tenders and stoker-fired. These massive engines are in two classes, those built by Mitsubishi in 1956 and the second class built by Mihara in 1963. They weigh over 100 tons and they look enormous machines for such a narrow gauge. Here is one of them being cleaned at Rio Gallegos for its afternoon run.

CHILE

Right: The Railways of Chile are built essentially on two gauges, the broad (5ft 6in) gauge of the state system running between Santiago, Valparaiso and points south, and the metre gauge lines in the north. In addition, there is the Transandine Railway which crosses under the Continental Divide at something over 10,450ft. The Transandine Railway on its steepest sections runs with rack assistance. A special form of the Abt system with three bars is used on the Chilean side and the gradients are as steep as 8 per cent. Here is a picture of the line in winter after the snow has been ploughed out.

Far right: This formidable piece of machinery at Los Andes at the base of the Chilean side of the Transandine Railway is a fabulous old Esslingen rack-and-adhesion 0-6-8-0 tank engine once used for propelling the snow ploughs on the Chilean side of the summit. The three leading axles connect with the cogs on the Abt system and the four axle truck behind directly connects with the rail surface. This giant was rarely in action but when it was it must have provided a tremendous sight of power, even 60 years after it was built.

Below: The Chilean Northern system which works north from Calera up to Antofagasta and the far regions of the north has now gone over to diesel traction, but in 1963 there was a large group of steam engines, mostly American-built, surviving at Calera. Here is one of the many 2-8-2s which ran this line waiting for cutting up in 1963.

Below right: Once again Trevor Rowe has found a real treasure for us, namely a sub-metric line in Chile and the only branch of its kind in the south. This shows the Saboya to Capitan Pastene Railroad, down south below Concepción, with a 2ft gauge train at Saboya waiting for the daily standard gauge train from the north. The locomotive shown is 0-8-0 tank No 5058.

FCTC

PERU/ECUADOR

A really spectacular rail run is that between Cuzco and along the valleys of the Pachar and the Urubamba Rivers to visit Machu Picchu. This runs over a great pass to the north of Cuzco at something like 12,500ft and then down through splendid mountain scenery to the river which becomes ultimately a tributary of the Amazon. Here is a railcar in the river valley in typical Andean country.

Right: Ecuador, oddly enough, operates its railways on the 3ft 6in gauge, whereas most of the narrow gauge in South America is 3ft. We always think engine No 1 is rather a find and here is engine No 1 of the old Ecuador Northern line which ran in the high altiplano northwards from Quito, the capital. The engine, when we saw her, was standing derelict in Quito yards and is a 4-6-0 built by Borsig.

COLOMBIA

Left: The railways of Colombia are very attractive. They have been put together into a national 3ft gauge system after the constituent parts had worked for many years independently. However, they are now all joined up together by the construction of one of the largest railways built anywhere during the last twenty-five years, the new 400 mile line linking the capital with the Atlantic coast. Here is a modern freight train on the Central Division which serves Bogotá, the capital, hauled by Belgian-built 2-8-2 No 65 at Zipaquirá. The engine was built by Tubize of Charleroi in 1951.

Above: This is a photograph on the Pacific Division which had its headquarters at Cali. The photograph shows a Baldwin-built 4-8-0 No 50 ready to take on water before hauling the afternoon passenger local from Cali to Santander. The locomotive dates from 1927.

Below left: The Antioquia system had its headquarters at Medellín and very agreeably allowed its engineers to embellish their machines if they wished. Here is 2-8-2 No 87 in Medellín yards with lining out and finish paid for by the engineer out of his own pocket as this engine was permanently assigned to him. The engine was built by Henschel in 1955.

Below: This disused monster is an old Kitson-Meyer articulated tank engine. These were built by Robert Stephenson in 1935 for the old Girardot Railway. She is shown lying in Bogotá shops in 1960 waiting for the scrap dealer.

BOLIVIA

Far left: One of the great railroad sights in the world was the departure twice a week of the enormous international train which left La Paz, the capital of Bolivia, on Thursdays and Sundays with the ultimate destination of some of its carriages Buenos Aires, 1,700 miles away. On other days of the week the train was restricted to internal traffic and not such a huge affair. On the day when we saw it in 1967, the train consisted of 22 coaches and four huge 4-8-2s to lift the 554 ton train from its starting point at La Paz up the 1 in 33 gradient for 17km to the altiplano 1,500ft above. These big metre gauge engines were built by Vulcan Foundry in 1954.

Top left: The city of La Paz, although at 11,000 to 12,000ft, is, in fact, in a big crater and the surrounding plains are 1,500 to 2,500ft higher. Inside the crater there are some considerable gradients, not only on the two metre gauge main lines which work down into the city but also on their branches. One of the two Shay geared-engines still survived in 1967 and were seen dashing around the yards at La Paz, although 60 years old. Here is Shay No 1, originally of the La Paz-Beni Railway which is now closed.

Below left: Bolivia until very recently had something like 100 steam engines and some powerful Garratts, 4-8-2 + 2-8-4, were on the roster. Here is an early morning shot of one of these engines leaving Oruro, which was originally owned by the La Paz-Arica Railway which ran out through Chile to the Pacific coast from the capital.

Middle left: The station pilot at La Paz when we visited it in 1967 was a British-built 2-8-4 tank engine built by Kitson of Leeds before World War I. Before the Bolivian National Railways were put together this was originally owned by the Antofagasta and Bolivia Railway which was an independent concern, British-owned, for many years. The picture shows the edge of the crater in which La Paz lies.

Below: Big metre gauge express engines were not common but here is an attractive American-built example which we believe was a free gift from Brazil to Bolivia when they became redundant from diesel working. These light 4-8-4s were fast and attractive engines. They were nicknamed 'bicycles' because of their speed.

BRAZIL

Above: Unfortunately the rather dowdy 3ft gauge Cantareira section of the metre gauge Sorocabana Railway at São Paulo is now closed. This line operated a suburban service with a whole fleet of Baldwin 4-6-0s, painted green with copper capped chimneys, dating from around 1910. Here is a group of them at their terminal waiting for the afternoon rush in 1963.

Right: A rather more respectable section of the Sorocabana Railway outside the electrified lines which served the suburban service of São Paulo is seen here. The photograph shows a passenger train with a modern Pacific at Capivari on the Jundiaí–Piracicaba line.

Below: Alas the metre gauge Fell line of the Leopoldina Railway in Brazil is no more, departing this life in 1965. The Fell section ran for eight miles and climbed the coastal mountains near Rio de Janeiro. The maximum gradient was 1 in 12½ and to climb it even with Fell assistance the train had to be broken up into very small sections, two coaches at the most. We regard a footplate ride on this as one of the really enjoyable experiences. Here is the train at its halfway point taking water behind one of the most modern of the Fell tank engines built by North British as recently as 1946.

Below right: Another casualty in the hills near Rio is the rack section of the Leopoldina line which climbed up to the old summer capital and resort of Petrópolis. The rack section on the Riggenbach system was 3¼ miles long with a maximum gradient of 1 in 5¼. The rack engines were Swiss, as is usual, and at one time as many as fourteen were in use. However, road traffic has destroyed the need for this line and all the inconveniences of breaking up trains to climb the hill. Here are two of the rack engines at Vila Inhomirim about 30 miles from Rio de Janeiro at the foot of the climb in 1963.

LEOPOLDINA
LEOPOLDINA

MEXICO

Far left: The San Lazaro terminus at Mexico City was a great place to visit in the forties, fifties and early sixties but alas the glory has now departed. Here is 3ft gauge 2-8-0 No 76 bearing the insignia of the Interoceanico Railway. This was a British-owned line which was absorbed into the national system, but its engines kept their lettering and numbers until the end.

Left: Jim Shaughnessy has a tremendous eye for composition. Look at this picture of National Railways of Mexico, ten-wheeler No 190 being serviced in the San Lázaro engine terminal at Mexico City to be ready for the noon departure of passenger train No 128 for Amecameca and Ozumba. Everything is right here, down to the hosing down of the boiler by the fireman.

Below: Here again is the San Lazaro terminal this time by night with the mixed track — 3ft and standard — showing. 2-8-0 No. 255 on the right is doing some switching while 2-8-0 No 76 is waiting for morning.

Above: The noon train northbound at Ozumba is crossing a bridge over a dry watercourse with the great volcano Ixtaccíhuatl in the background. The locomotive is 4-6-0 No 190 and some attractive old coaches are part of the consist.

Right: A southbound freight train waiting at Nepantla for the afternoon train up out of Cuautla. In this picture the volcano Popocatépetl can be seen in the background. As can be seen here no money was wasted on ballasting the 3ft gauge track. The picture dates from the early sixties.

Below: Cuautla station, one of the last narrow gauge centres of the National Railways of Mexico. The two nearest locomotives are No 260, which is a Baldwin 4-6-0 used for mixed trains, and 2-8-0 No 269, while in the distance is Interoceanico 2-8-0 No 74. It is high noon in summer. The hot sun beats down and nobody feels very strenuous.

Below right: Here comes a narrow gauge freight battling up the Ozumba Hill northbound out of Cuautla on its way towards Mexico City. The 2-8-0s are really working hard. The brakemen on the roofs of the freight cars now have a moment to take it easy.

Above left: National Railways of Mexico: a mixed train between Cuautla and Puente de Ixtla shown on its afternoon run between the two towns as it approaches San Carlos station. The locomotive is 2-8-0 No 70 in FCI livery. The old flat-topped coaches are as old as the locomotive or more. This branch was the last steam operation in Mexico.

Above: Here is one of the authors enjoying himself on the footplate of Baldwin 4-6-0 No 186 on a run from Mexico City to Amecameca in 1962. The oil fire rumbled and roared, the exhaust beat clear and sharp and the great chime whistle reverberated in the hills, a day to remember.

Far left: Here is another picture at Cuautla showing three 2-8-0s waiting for passenger trains in 1960. On the left is Baldwin 2-8-0 No 269 built in 1921, then No 73 a Kerr Stuart 2-8-0 from Scotland built in 1904 for the British-owned Interoceanico line. Finally, on the right is another FCI 2-8-0, No 70, built by the American Locomotive Company at Schenectady in 1899.

Middle left: For a few years after the war a 2ft gauge section of the Mexicano Railway survived, the Huatusco branch in the province of Vera Cruz. There were two light Baldwin 2-6-0s which ran this service and here is one of them at Córdoba.

Bottom left: For a time the 3ft gauge lines in Mexico sported some huge Mallets with a 2-6-6-2 wheel arrangement. These big engines disappeared during the 1950s with the conversion to standard gauge of the section for which they were built south of Mexico City. These engines were built by Alco as recently as 1938.

Right: Another night scene at Cuautla with the fireman of 2-8-0 No 271 operating the injector before the train takes off for Ozumba Hill on the night run to Mexico City. The protruding firebox on this class of engine was highly inconvenient.

Far right: The noon train to Ozumba leaving Chalco after a water stop on the run down from Mexico City. The locomotive is a Baldwin-built 4-6-0.

Below: A passenger train leaving Los Reyes on a Mexico City-Ozumba local in the last days of steam in December 1965 behind 2-8-0 No 272. The line was taken over by diesel working in the spring of 1967.

190

Right: Puente de Ixtla passenger train leaving Oacalco on December 9th, 1965 on the 3ft gauge. In the summer of 1967 this engine and the three cars shown made the last steam passenger run in Mexico from Puente de Ixtla to Cuautla.

Far right: The F.C. Mineral de Chihuahua 2-8-0 No 7 working a train of loaded hopper wagons bound for the ore tippler at Santa Eulalia. The picture dates from 1963.

Below: The United Railways of Yucatán continued to operate steam well into the 1960s and amongst their attractive stock was a number of small 3ft gauge 4-4-0s and 2-6-0s, including two of the last 4-4-0s built in America dating from as recently as 1945. The picture here shows a rather older Baldwin 4-4-0 No 68 at Mérida in 1953. This one was built in 1923.

Below right: The Yucatán Railways Terminal at Mérida showing standard gauge 4-4-0 No 7 at the head of a train for Progreso, while on the mixed track next door a 3ft gauge train is waiting to take off for the back country behind a minute 2-6-0 *Dignity and Impudence*. This photo dates from 1962.

NICARAGUA/HONDURAS/
GUATEMALA

Left: F.C. del Pacifico de Nicaragua 2-8-0 No 28 (Alco) works eastward along the shore of Lake Managua with mixed No 1 between Miraflores and Bella Vista. The train runs between Corinto and Granada and was the only one to cover the entire 117 mile main line; 3ft 6in gauge.

Top: The Tela Railroad of Honduras is owned by one of the two fruit companies operating there. Here is an engineer oiling his locomotive during the course of a long stop at Toloa Empalme. The train is No 22 westbound from Tela to Baracoa Empalme in May 1962, and the locomotive is a Baldwin war-surplus 2-8-2.

Above: The railway in Guatemala has some considerable freight traffic dealing with the United Fruit Company's shipments to both Atlantic and Pacific coasts, and until the mid-1960s there were plenty of modern outside-frame 2-8-2s built since World War II. Here is one of the most recent locomotives of this class at Guatemala City in 1961.

Left: The sugar plantations have for many years been the home of attractive little steam engines, though this day is now passing and diesels or motor vehicles are taking their place. In Antigua there was something like 50 miles of 2ft 6in gauge track all serving the sugar fields and as late as 1960 we managed to find some Kerr Stuart 0-4-2 tanks built for this service. Here is *Lena* looking rather down at heel but still capable of steaming. One of these engines has just been purchased for the Welshpool and Llanfair Railway.

Below left: There are some sugar railways in Haiti also, working under the attractive name of the 'Compagnie de la Plaine du Cul-de-Sac', a 2ft 6in gauge line which had some decidedly decrepit wood-fired steam engines. Here is one of them at Port-au-Prince in 1960.

Below: The state railway of Haiti runs on 3ft 6in gauge and some sort of a ramshackle mixed service has been maintained for years. In this picture Baldwin 4-6-0 No 3 wheezes quietly at the terminus at Port-au-Prince, having brought in a mixed train with a number of fruit wagons and a few passengers. The picture dates from 1960.

Africa

In Europe and America one thinks of narrow gauge railways as oddities which are on the way out. But in the rest of the world matters are otherwise, and except in the north the standard railway gauge in the continent of Africa is 3ft 6in, or one metre in East Africa. These lines flourish, with heavy and increasing freight and passenger traffic: and especially on the lines originally built by the British one can still travel in some style.

Somehow there is something rather special about a sleeping-car anywhere, be it British Rail's to places like Inverness, or the Wagon-Lits Company's magnificent vehicles to Paris, Vienna or Istanbul. There is just the same feeling on the East African Railways' Mombasa to Nairobi express, now diesel-hauled by the new 90 class locomotives. The train leaves Mombasa in the early evening and within a few minutes you pass the loco shed on the right hand side, still with some red Garratts, almost all of them with the flat Giesl Ejector chimney. Soon it is time for dinner in a really comfortable car with fresh flowers on the tables and pleasant, courteous service, and by the time the delicious meal is over it is dark and the beds are made up. Morning finds the train with its loco growling hard up the gradients, close to the borders of the Nairobi Game Park and many kinds of wild creatures are standing about watching it go by. Less luxurious but more evocative, the interested traveller may have an opportunity of riding on the footplate of one of the huge 59 class 4-8-2 + 2-8-4s, oil burners whose cabs are as clean as the bridge of a steamship. There is no doubt that East Africa, at present, is a rail lover's paradise, for what more can one want than a mixture of steam, sun, wild animals and a welcome. However, even here time is running out for steam — the World Bank has authorised a loan for the building of new diesels.

But it is almost certainly South Africa which attracts the lion's share of railway enthusiast visitors, for here are over 13,000 miles of 3ft 6in gauge track, and nearly 300 miles of the narrow 2ft lines — and there is still plenty of steam to be seen on both. In fact, as recently as 1968, some new Garratts were constructed for the 2ft gauge and are used on the Natal branches. They were built in South Africa by Hunslet Taylor Consolidated (Pty) Ltd. On the 3ft 6in gauge, steam is now slowly on the decline but the huge 4-8-4s, condensing and non-condensing, built by North British and Henschel in the mid-1950s are still going strong. Connected to the South African metals are those of the Rhodesia Railways, first seen by one of us on active service during World War II. Here there are more Garratts working as well as other types, and Bulawayo shed alone is well worth visiting if one can get there. It is strange to think that only a few years ago British

engine drivers were being asked to go out to Rhodesia to help with the shortage of those technicians! Steam, whether Garratts or 4-8-2s, is used on a large number of passenger trains and indeed the 'mail' from Bulawayo to Victoria Falls is steam hauled throughout.

Other countries in Africa still have plenty of steam power, except those which were originally French or whose railways were under French influence such as Ethiopia. But though the railways may be there, they are often difficult to get at and even more difficult to photograph. In the west, Nigeria is not yet a tourist area, particularly after its civil war, and in the North Cameroons you will certainly not be welcome. How one envies that American oil man and excellent descriptive writer, Charles Small who, only ten years back published his book *Far Wheels* (Cleaver Hume Press Ltd). Duty and service took him all over the world from Japan to Mozambique, Port Sudan to Peru, and everywhere he went he sought out and rode on the local trains. Nowhere more so than in Africa, where he took in the civilised East African Railways in detail, along with the not so accessible Ferrovié Eritrée, the Chemin de Fer Franco-Ethiopien, and the lines of the Belgian Congo and Madagascar — all beyond the normal tourist's dreams to-day. Now many of the pages of his book are historical reading.

The survival of so much steam in South Africa has to do with South African politics — the country has no oil, but cheap and abundant coal, and a reluctance to depend on imported fuel! As in most other African countries, freight moves pretty exclusively by rail, and road haulage is subject to strict limitation, so the maintenance of the railway system in a state of self-sufficient good health is an important matter. Many main lines are electrified, and there are a fair number of diesels, particularly on secondary lines in arid areas, or areas with peculiarly difficult grades and tunnel problems. But the SAR still have nearly 2,000 steam engines hard at work, well-maintained and doing the job they were designed to do; and to spend a few hours by the lineside anywhere between, for instance, Kimberley and Beaufort West on the Cape Town to Johannesburg main line, to see a continual procession of huge 4-8-4s with enormous condensing tenders come storming past, was a refreshing experience. Passenger trains tend to be rather slow (often still running to their original nineteenth-century timings) but are still comfortable, and quite well filled. But freight trains are operated with great efficiency, and often rather faster! Even the 2ft gauge branches are prosperous and for the moment entirely steampowered although diesels are on order for the Cape Province line. These sections, in fact, operate no scheduled passenger services but it is possible to arrange for a coach to be added to one of the freight trains between Port Elizabeth and Loerie.

There cannot be many locomotive depots left in the world with over 100 active steam engines based there, and seldom sound nor smell of a diesel. But there are several on the South African and Rhodesian Railways; and, putting politics aside (for the best way to understand these things is to experience them) every steam fanatic who can possibly make the trip should do so before it is too late: for even there main line steam is living on borrowed time.

Above left: At 9.20 every morning two trains left Bloemfontein, the capital of the Orange Free State, simultaneously. The train on the left behind a 15E Pacific, its tender piled with Witbank coal, is bound for Durban; the train on the right, headed by a 15F 4-8-2, is a slow or semi-fast train for Cape Town.

Above: The 25th anniversary of the 'Blue Train', the great express which plies between Johannesburg and Cape Town, was celebrated in April 1969 by an all-steam special run. This brought the crowds out and was indeed a triumphant success. Here is the train leaving Johannesburg behind a 15E Pacific with rotary cam valve gear.

Left: Big power. Mainline freight train fighting the grade behind two class 25C 4-8-4 condensing engines. With these the tender is longer than the engine and all-up they weigh some 235 tons. While naturally like all condensing engines these are something of a box of tricks, they have turned out reasonably well in the arid areas of the Republic and can run up to 500 miles without a water stop.

Below: Here in typical Free State scenery, the vast illimitable veldt with no trees for miles, a 15E Mountain class is pulling a huge train of brick-red and cream painted carriages from Kroonstad to Durban via Harrismith in May 1968.

Right: If you like the dry countryside of South Africa, often semi-desert or desert, then it attracts most powerfully. Here on the old Cape Midland main line a freight starts its weary climb up the Carlton Bank to Naupoort in July 1966. The engine is a 4-8-2 of class 15BR.

Far right: Still in Cape Province and still from the able camera of Allen Jorgensen here is a freight attacking the Lotsborg Incline behind Class 19BR 4-8-2, the only survivor of its family. The train runs from Rosmead to Graaf Reinet; date July 1968.

Below right: In its big locomotive stud the SAR until recently still had room for some charming old veterans like the 7M class 4-8-0 which, with its light axle load, could be used on the flimsiest of branch lines. Here in the evening light and in the evening of its life old 987 creeps across the veldt towards Touws River in March 1967. This was a once-a-week run for the veteran as normally a modern light 2-8-4 of the 24th class was in charge.

Below: The South African Railways still have 1993 steam locomotives at the time of writing, so the end of steam is a long way off here, for reasons as much strategic as economic. Among the most attractive and successful group of locomotives is the family of 15F class 4-8-2s which are seen everywhere and on all sorts of jobs.

Right: Here is another 15F, this time at the head of a big iron-ore train leaving De Aar junction, bound for the coast at Port Elizabeth and thence for Japan. The early morning light here shows up the narrow gauge track sharply.

Far right: The repair shops of the South African Electricity Supply Company are at Rosherville, a few miles east of Johannesburg. Here they have the nice idea of keeping a couple of old steam engines to do the yard work and these two, now called *Kitson* and *Barclay,* take alternate days unless you are very favoured and then both are in steam. *Kitson,* a 4-6-0, was built for the Natal Government Railways in 1879, while *Barclay* was built in 1907 for the Jersey Railways and Tramways who named her *La Moye.* She came out to Africa from the Channel Islands in 1928 and is still as pretty an engine as you could find anywhere. Both are impeccably kept with chocolate paint lined-out in red. We drove both of them and old *Kitson* stole the show; as smooth as silk, she ran like a watch.

Below: Although many miles of 2ft gauge in south-west Africa have now been converted to the Cape Gauge of 3ft 6in, several flourishing lines survive on the east coast. The most famous of these is the Port Elizabeth-Avontuur line in Cape Province which runs 225 miles in from the coast over steep gradients, fierce curves and now and again, as the picture shows, a deep river gorge. The country is fertile and prosperous and the line handles a big trade in apples and timber. The engines are 4-8-2s and small Garratts. Diesels are on order alas!

Below right: Here is a picture on the Avontuur 2ft gauge line with one of the sturdy little 2-6-2 + 2-6-2 Garratts at the head of a mixed train. Further up the coast at Umzinto in Natal we came across another group of these little engines; they are now hard pressed for already the work, mostly sugar and timber haulage, has brought about an increase in the locomotive stud from nine to eighteen in ten years and more power is needed. As recently as 1967 and 1968 a batch of these engines was built from the Beyer Peacock design by Hunslet of South Africa. But diesels have now arrived at Port Elizabeth.

RHODESIA/MASHONALAND

Top right: No 122, one of a small series of 4-8-0s with 4ft wheels built in 1916 by the American Locomotive Company. Photographed at Bulawayo in 1944.

Middle right: No 80 is a 4-8-0 built in 1912 by Beyer Peacock rebuilt in 1939 with larger boiler to increase tractive effort from 25,500 to 27,000 lb. This engine has 4ft wheels. Photographed at Bulawayo in 1944.

Far right: No 7 *Jacktar.* This was the only named locomotive on the RR&M system, an 0-6-0T with 2ft 9in wheels, it was built in 1896 by Manning Wardle and rebuilt in 1927. When photographed in 1944 she was Workshop shunter at Bulawayo. She is now preserved.

Below: Somabula at 4,638ft above sea level must be an attractive place to live climatically. The railway lines do a brisk trade internally and with South Africa to the south, Mozambique to the east and surprisingly until recently with Zambia to the north.

Below right: In Rhodesia locomotive driving is mainly white man's work, though in other parts of the continent, Africans have taken to it with success. Here is the front end of 4-8-0 No 80 at Bulawayo, the headquarters of the RR, about to be cleaned out.

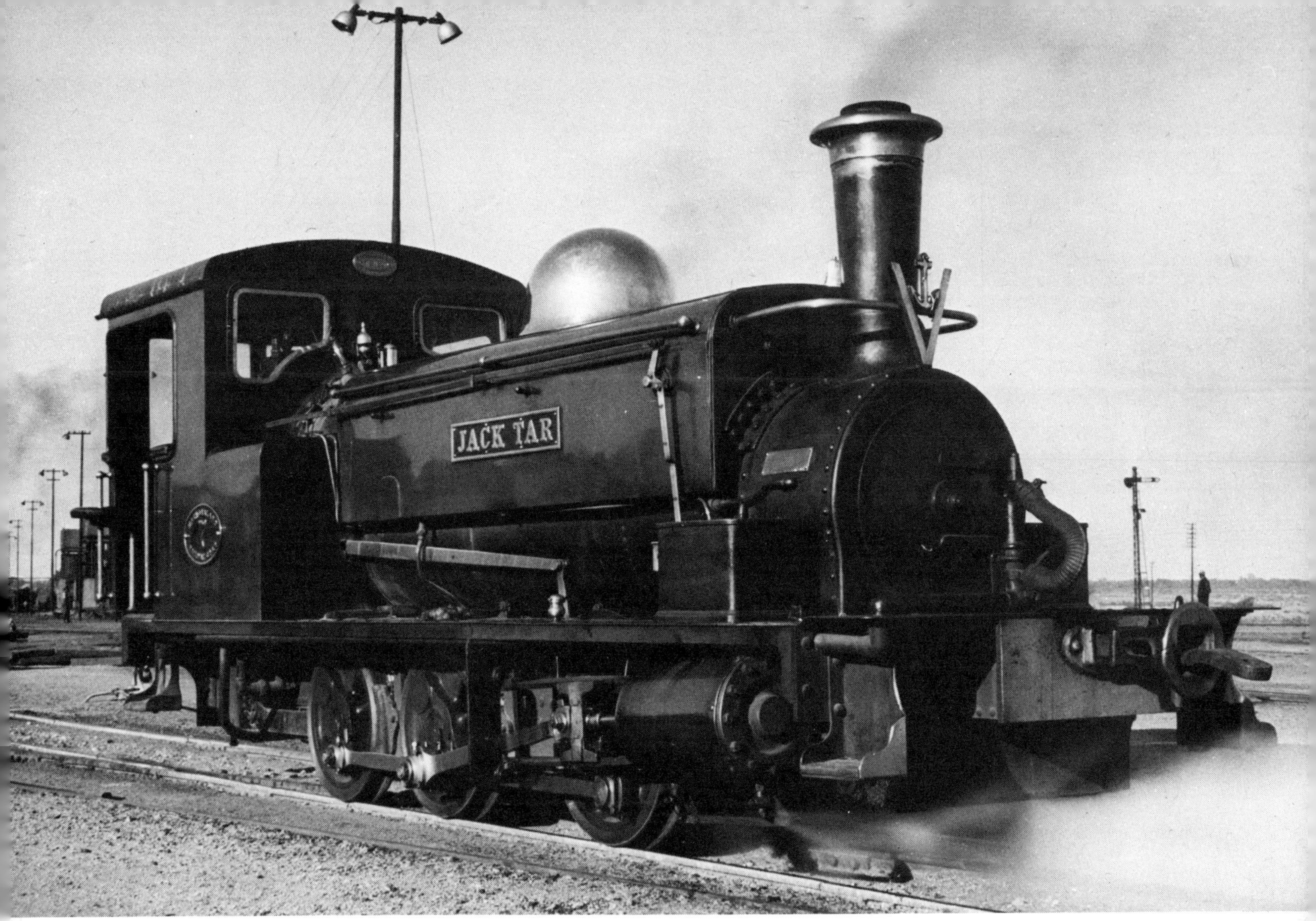
JACK TAR

SOMABULA
4638 FEET ABOVE SEA LEVEL

No

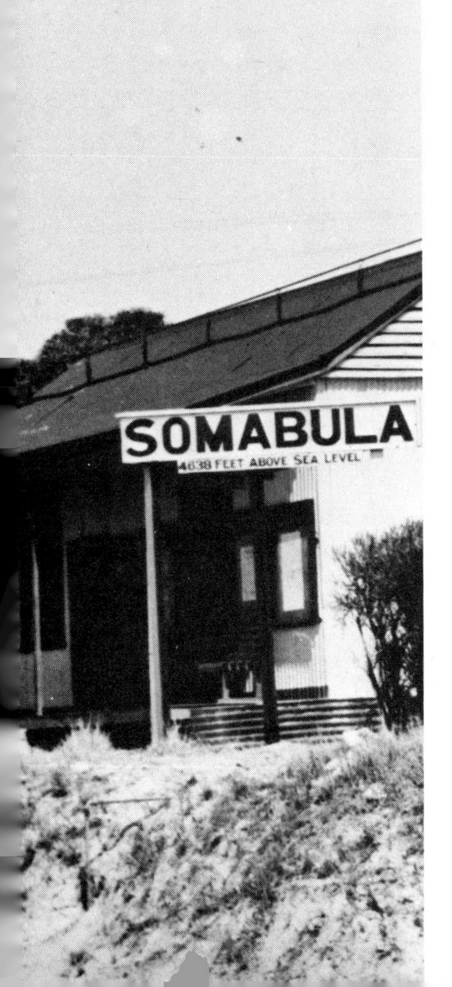

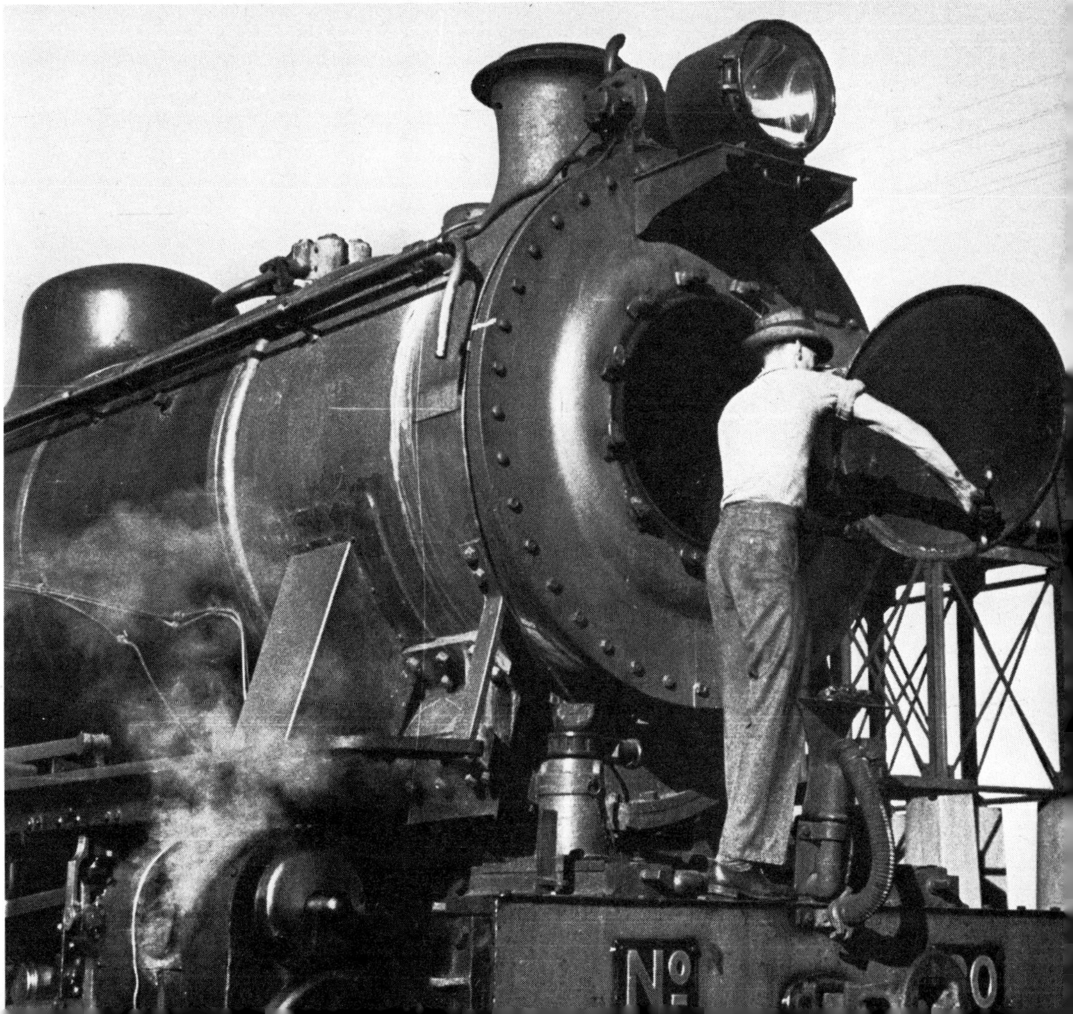

Top right: The 'Pride of the Shed'! Class 15 4-6-4 + 4-6-4 Garratt No 400 stands gleaming outside the Bulawayo Shed in July 1971

Middle right: Smaller Garratt, 2-6-2 + 2-6-2 No 503 at Salisbury Shed in July 1971. Note the overhead water gantry, a feature rarely seen in Europe.

Far right: 2OA, 705 rests in Victoria Falls station before shunting and continuing to Livingstone in Zambia.

Below: 4-8-0 No 110 with a goods train in the sidings near Bulawayo Shed in July 1971.

Below right: Without any doubt the Victoria Falls is one of the really great sights of the world. The best way to see it is from an aeroplane for then one can see clearly the deep narrow slot into which the wide Zambezi falls and the incredibly narrow gorge which carries away all the water which was so widely spread before. The best sight of all is when a train rumbles over the bridge to add to nature's bounty. Here is an old 4-8-2 hauling a freight over into Zambia.

SWAZILAND

Swaziland has recently obtained its independence from Britain and now own a short railway line with ex-SAR stock to run it; its *raison d'être* is to haul iron ore. In other ways Swaziland is most sophisticated with a hotel and country club and even a casino to tempt visitors from the austerities of South Africa.

MOZAMBIQUE

The railways of Mozambique, as Portuguese East Africa is now called, are delightful and many pleasant surprises await the researcher. In five days he found 83 steam engines of 27 different classes in December 1970. The systems out of the two main ports of Lourenco Marques and Beira tie in with the South African and Rhodesia Railways and now the northern line from Nampula connects with Malawi, so much through traffic is carried. Here is a Henschel 2-8-2 built in the 1950s heading a passenger train near Lourenco Marques.

Far right: It was something of a surprise to find Canadian-built engines in Lourenco Marques but a group of 4-8-2s was supplied just after the war by the now defunct Montreal Locomotive Works. These were later supplemented by a batch of Henschel engines, handsome Pacifics, Mikados and Santa Fes. All of these were going strong in late 1970.

Below: It was Charles Small who put the 75cm gauge Linha de Gaza on the map for us, as he discovered it and wrote it up in *Far Rails*. It runs inland from Joao Belo on the Limpopo river about 75 miles north of Lourenco Margues. Here is an American Locomotive Co 2-6-0 built in 1919 at Cooke Works for the Quelimane Railway; she still survived in 1970.

Below right: Without a doubt we think this picture should get the prize for Africa if not the world for it shows one of the last four Atlantics left, the remainder of a huge line of fast flyers, elegant passenger engines—the apotheosis of 1913 in a sense. In fact these engines are rather later as they were built by Henschel in 1923. We made a special pilgrimage to Nampula to find these engines and even managed to get a brief ride on the footplate of No 813, this very engine. The photograph shows 4-4-2 No 813 arriving at Nampula with a train from the port of Nacala near to Mozambique city in the north of the province. This class was still operating in 1975.

ANGOLA

Left: Portugal had wide territories on the west side of Africa in Angola and one notable railway, the Benguela, British-built and British-operated, runs right across the province to link up with the railways for Zaïre and the Copper Belt of Zambia. The Benguela Railway has a stock of Garratts and rather unusually most are wood-burning. Here is one at the head of a freight train crossing a passenger train at Vila Verde.

Below left: Here is another winner, this time of the isolated 3ft 6in gauge Quelimane line which runs up from the coast in the centre of the coastline of Mozambique. Here we see Baldwin 2-8-2 (built in 1948) leaving Quelimane with a mixed train for Macuba while two Henschel 2-8-2s sit and simmer on the right. All the engines on this line are wood-fired and the traffic is sisal and timber.

Below: Much of the Benguela line (3ft 6in gauge) runs over high tableland having come up from the coast on some fierce gradients. One section was built for rack operation but this has been discontinued. Here is one of the ubiquitous Garratts on a mixed train near the coast.

Left: When a Garratt is not needed there's a 4-8-2 for the job in Angola. Here is one on the Benguela Railway heading for the port of Lobito from Catumbela station.

Below: Further north in Angola another line runs inland on 3ft 6in gauge from Luanda, the capital, into the interior at Malanje. We explored a little of this strange empty land including a run down an abominable side road which nearly destroyed our car, amid myriads of butterflies, through the uninhabited jungle to see the 2ft gauge line branching off the main line at Canhoca to run up to Golungo Alto. Here the bad road made us miss the daily passenger train which was hauled by 0-6-2 tank with a copper-capped chimney, but rewarded us with this old 0-8-0 veteran built in 1922 by Orenstein & Koppel.

Middle: The most modern engines on the Angola lines out of Luanda are these Jung 2-8-2s built about fifteen years ago.

With black paint, red chassis and wheels and some brightwork, these engines look well at the head of a rake of crimson coaches which may well be 50 years old.

Bottom: Needless to say, there are Garratts on the northern Angola line, some like this one from Beyer Peacock of Manchester and others from Krupps. Today, however, they are rarely used, as the ubiquitous diesel has taken over.

EAST AFRICA

Above: The East African Railways serve Kenya, Tanzania and Uganda with their headquarters in Nairobi. They run on metre gauge unlike all the other British and Portuguese-built railways in Africa which use 3ft 6in. Steam is in retreat here with an increasing number of diesels and more to come. Garratts are plentiful and so too are Giesl ejectors which have been fitted widely. Here is a Garratt at the head of a mixed train on the Nile bridge at Jinja in Uganda.

Above right: This is the special Royal train used by the Queen Mother in 1959 near Kikuyu in Kenya. It is here drawn by two Beyer Peacock 60 class Garratts which are of the 4-8-4 + 4-8-4 wheel arrangement. The train consists of seventeen cars in all.

Right: Both of the authors had the good luck to get a footplate ride out of Nairobi on a 59 class 4-8-2 + 2-8-4 Garratt in November 1969 at the head of a considerable freight train. Mr Mwalumbi, the African driver, kindly gave up his seat and said ''It's all yours'' and what fun that was. The 59 class weigh 250 tons and are the biggest surviving steam engines in the world we believe, unless there is something bigger still in service in Russia.

Far middle right: Back in 1946 it all ran under another name—the Kenya and Uganda Railway. Steam was supreme, all drivers were Europeans and Dr Giesl still unknown. Here is a 4-8-4 + 4-8-4 of EAR 58 class leaving Nairobi with a northbound train.

Far bottom right: The 4-8-0s were still numerous and at work on the KUR in the mid 1940s and surviving at the end of the 60s. Here is a southbound train entering Nairobi in March 1946.

WEST AFRICA

Above left: The Nigerian Railways before the Civil War of 1965 and the subsequent troubles were a well-run, efficient organisation with steam slowly giving way to diesels. A most successful class of 2-8-2 mixed traffic engine was the River class built by Armstrong Whitworth in the 1940s and 1950s. Here is No 126 *River Oni* at Kaduna in 1960.

Above: The Garratt was not absent in Nigeria though there were not very many of them; here is Double Pacific No 517 at Kano in northern Nigeria in 1965.

Far left: The new line in Ghana to the new port of Tema was celebrated by a special train carrying the prime minister of what was then the Gold Coast; this was in 1954. Since then, Nkrumah, the Redeemer, has come and gone and the steam engines have been largely replaced by diesels. Pacific No 364 does the honours and supports the Arms of Britain.

Left: The Sierra Leone Railways run on the 2ft 6in gauge with an invigorating start up the main street of Freetown. Here is a 1954 picture of a passenger train with a 4-8-0 at the head crossing the famous curved, sloping bridge at Hastings about fourteen miles from the capital.

NORTH AFRICA

Far left: On the waterfront at Benghazi an Italian 0-4-4-0 Mallet tank moves out with a freight train. These lines in Libya run on the odd Italian narrow gauge of 95cm.

Left: On the same set of rails ran these wooden bogie coaches better to look at than to ride in. Steam hauled in 1950 it was worth braving the heat and the sand for a ride on what has now become part of history.

Below: Those who served in North Africa during the 1939/45 war will have many memories of Cairo and Alexandria. When we were lucky it was possible to take a few days off by the sea at Alex and on the way from Cairo we would meet the 2ft 6in gauge trains of the Nile Delta Railway. Here is one of the Sentinel steam tram engines on a passenger train.

India and Asia

This huge area stretching from Turkey to Japan embraces a multitude of railways and a large proportion of narrow gauge. India alone has over 15,500 miles of metre gauge, about as much as of broad gauge, and 2,670 miles of 2ft 6in and 2ft lines as well; of these last, more in a moment.

Setting out West to East we find a small section of narrow gauge in Turkey, and some more in Syria, the Lebanon and Iraq. Jordan with the Hedjaz Railway continues the lines south from Syria, and the plan is to continue into Saudi Arabia, but not on the old road bed where Colonel Lawrence's Arabs had worked havoc in the 1914 war.

Iran has nothing for us now; East Pakistan, now Bangladesh, had over half its tracks in metre gauge and West Pakistan has its narrow gauge lengths on its eastern frontier, but strangely enough, the rails through the Khyber Pass are on 5ft 6in standard. Leaving India aside for the moment, we come next to Burma, which we were only able to visit too late to make the deadline for this book; the metre gauge there supports some modern British built 2-6-4 tanks and 2-8-2s and Pacifics built just after World War II.

China is almost entirely standard gauge country, except that we believe that in the extreme western province of Yunnan there is some metre gauge dating from the period of French Imperialism in Indo-China.

From Indo-China, although we have nothing to offer from Laos and Cambodia, we have managed to get some pictures from Vietnam, including a scene on the rack.

In Thailand and Malaya the metre gauge has all its own way, and steam still had until recently a large part to play; the elegant Pacifics in both countries were a pleasure to see.

Indonesia, which we visited for the first time in 1970, showed us some fine 3ft 6in gauge veterans, 4-6-4 well tanks from Dutch Imperial times, an elderly 2-6-0 tank to ride on, and even a 4-4-0 from the last century. This, as more recent and wide ranging travellers tell us, is still a real steam paradise with huge Mallets and diminutive tram engines.

The Philippines are unknown territory first hand, but a brief stop in Taiwan in 1970 revealed some vestigial steam on the 3ft 6in gauge, in the shape of Japanese engines and we have just seen some splendid pictures of 3-cylinder Shays on the 2ft 6in Mount Ali Forest Railway. South Korea is on 4ft 8½in though some steam survives, and so we come to Japan, a big narrow gauge territory.

Here the railway is big business, and so alas, steam is gone

and electrification is advancing.

Then in Japan the 4ft 8½in super-express lines are coming more into the picture. The Tokaido line from Tokyo to Kobe with three or four trains an hour is an established success, though strangely disappointing as a speedway; the double windows and the welded rail combine to cut out the sounds of speed so that 125mph seems like no more than a prosaic 80.

So back to India where steam has still a huge part to play on all gauges in the national economy. I think we cannot do better than quote our friend Mike Satow a former managing director of ICI India, and an indefatigable researcher into obscure Indian railways. He has not only surveyed the strange monorail relics in Central India but has also found a coal railway in Eastern Assam with a rare assortment of old steam engines including eleven Bagnalls with four different types of valve gear and a coal pit shaft which runs up into the hillside instead of down into the earth's bowels. However, let him speak for himself.

Two and a half rupees buys a coloured Indian Railway guide map, a microcosm of the third largest railway system in the world; more than 1,000 miles North to South and East to West, and with 116 years of history and tradition behind it. Study the map closely, and you will discern amongst the varying colours of the different regions lines of differing weight, the broad 5ft 6in gauge; the medium metre-gauge, and, interwoven, the little fine lines which add up to the 2,500 odd miles of light (2ft 6in) and the narrow (2ft 0in) gauge railways. Spend another three rupees and you will be the possessor of the current month's edition of Newman's Indian Bradshaw which devotes the first 250 pages to the Indian railway scene and, as a rather surprising bonus, a further fifty on the Pakistan and Ceylon railways! To any lover of steam, there is more than a feast to be found on the light and narrow gauges, and a study of Bradshaw will yield over fifty timetables from which to make a selection.

To visit and record the entire narrow gauge scene of India, scattered as it is over 1,000 miles in each direction, could be a full-time job with the possibility that some of it has withered or died by the time one gets there. Happily, however, some of the more exciting of the narrow gauge railway workings are not too remote from the beaten track, and what follows are some of the impressions which I have been able to gain in the odd moments when there has been time to deviate from the routine paths and journey more sedately by what, to me, is still the most fascinating means of transport. I have had the fortune to visit — by accident or design — some of the more interesting of these lines. Some are of international fame, others unknown and overtaken by time struggle on through the thickening jungle of competition knowing only too well that the ultimate end of the line is drawing close. It is the mountain railways (modestly described in official documents as Hill Railways, though three of them climb to over 7,000ft!) which tend to steal the limelight from the point of view of

sheer grandeur of scene, civil engineering achievement and hard work by the locomotive stock, but there is much on the plains to fascinate the keen observer, even if only because of a sudden and unexpected discovery, all too often when one is travelling on official business with its demands on time and schedule! No one could register excitement over the working of the Bankura-Rainagar line, with its sixty miles of level and largely straight track through the West Bengal countryside laid with 35lb. F.B. rail from Barrow and Roy-Marklew patent joints. Three trains a day, a forlorn selection of rolling stock, some fitted with the Marklew patent corrugated axle journals, and a few weary Bagnall 2-6-2 and 0-6-4 tank locos make up the scene. Driving through Bankura on the second day of 1970, I came across a 2ft 6in gauge level crossing and promptly altered course to head for the station. Here were rakes of tattered 4- and 8-wheel coaches, wood seated, unlighted, unglazed, unpainted. No locos — no pulse. I walked off down the track, over the level crossing and 100 yards away round a bend in the track appeared No. 10, one of the last (1953) Bagnalls with bits of patchwork welded over the leaks in the side tanks. Round a spur to the right and I was in the workshops — two abandoned 'Sentinels' in front of me and an incredible collection of ancient relics and machines. Has any of my readers visited a machine shop recently where the line shafting is driven by an agricultural overtype portable single-cylinder steam engine in the middle of the shop, with the original two-cylinder one abandoned years ago still standing beside it? And then noticed that there was no water in the gauge glass—and no fire in the firebox? "No Sir—the boiler was condemned some years ago, now the steam comes from our new boiler!" which turned out to be an ancient Cochrane, belching smoke and connected by 60 feet of unlagged $1\frac{1}{2}$ inch piping!

Then there is the 2ft 6in Shahdara/Sharanpur outside Delhi and running due north for about 100 miles. Flat and monotonous as a journey unless you are on the footplate of one of the old Hunslet 2-6-2 or 2-6-4 tanks. What a ride! I did a tape recording on one of these not long ago and by way of laying on the effect, the driver worked her up to at least the limit of 30mph for piped trains. (The pipes were there all right, but I can't recollect any continuity being established!) The clatter drowned any attempt at commentary and I ended up clutching my equipment and camera and hoping we would still be on the footplate at the first stop! The extensive little 2ft 0in gauge Howrah-Amta and Howrah-Sheakhala wanders generally westwards from Calcutta. Another busy, tired, unprofitable little railway with motive power by Hunslet, Avonside and Manning-Wardle. No money for paint, hardly enough for repairs, but still busy and handling upwards of 8 million passengers each year at absurdly low fares while the buses roar past and overtake on the adjacent road.

And so it is all over this vast land. Driving from Bangalore to Kolar Gold Fields a few weeks ago, my eye chanced on a large polished brass steam dome moving sedately in the opposite direction behind a clump of shrubs some 200 yards away. There was no time to stop and pursue, but now I know that the Bangalore-Bangarapet railway is still in service!

Up to the hills and since we have moved south, let me recall the only rack railway in India; the metre gauge line which connects Mettupalaiyam on the plains with Ootaca-mund some 7278ft up in the Nilagiri Hills. This is a fine railway, set amongst superb wooded slopes with enchanting little stations bearing improbable English names: Runnymead, Wellington, Lovedale, amongst others of more local association and origin, all clean and gay with bougainvillaea and potted plants. On one occasion I was escorting an important visitor who is also a great railway enthusiast. We were to be guests of the railway and drove down to Runneymead to await train No 528, which we were to join for the journey up to Coonoor and Aravankadu. We were received with traditional hospitality by the stationmaster and his staff of two; the station immaculate; flowers in profusion and refreshments and clean napkins in his office. 'No — we hardly ever have a passenger at this station now — but we have to keep it open — it's the last watering point before Coonoor', was his sad comment. Looking at his gross station receipts neatly charted on the wall and showing monthly figures of around Rs. 40/-, I felt moved to purchase two first-class singles from Runneymead to Aravankadu which at Rs. 9/- each must have offset the cost of his hospitality and even shown a peak for February 1969!

Close to its booked time came the soft roar of the train approaching with the engine working compound on the rack. The coaching stock is smart in its blue and white livery, clean and comfortable, and on the 'expresses' a fine observation compartment leads the train up the hill, with the loco always 'below' and pushing, as a safeguard against coupling failure. Seven coaches, totalling about 90 tons gross with one of the fine 49-ton class 'X' 0-8-2 tank locos, built by the Swiss Locomotive Works, in two almost identical batches in 1920 and 1952, nosed into the station and came to rest with the loco under the water tower. These machines are beautifully designed and built, and well maintained.

Cab layout is complex in the extreme. Steam and vacuum brakes, separate hand brakes for adhesion and rack regulator, L.P. starter, reverser, interceptor, compression releases for each engine when running downhill and using compressive braking, boiler water injection to cylinders to assist cylinder lubrication and temperature control under compressibe braking and all the usual accoutrements. Riding on the footplate is an impressive and rewarding experience. The track is in excellent alignment, fitted with P & M track lubricators, and the whole atmosphere is one of efficiency and traditional pride. From Ooty in the South to Darjeeling in the North-East is a long hop which provides a dramatic contrast from the gentle wooded heights of the Nilagiris to the rugged splendour of the Himalayas, and an equal contrast in railways. From the relatively expansive metre gauge and the fine powerful SLM locos of the South we come upon the diminutive 2ft gauge of the Darjeeling Himalayan railway with its stud of 29 little 14 ton 0-4-0 Sharp Stewart and North British locos (with one interloper supplied in 1917 by Baldwin to the same design) — for all the world like hill ponies struggling their way up 1:25 and even 1:19 at one spot, twisting and turning and looping with their 32 tons permitted load behind them. As a guest of the railway, my last visit was indeed memorable. I had ridden the line from end to end on previous occasions; this time I drove up to Tindaria, 20 miles up the track from the terminus on the plain at Siliguri, and was received by the Executive Engineer and the Assistant Mechanical Engineer in charge of the shops. The shops are ancient and efficient. There are ferrous and non-ferrous foundries, forge, machine and fitting bays. They make everything, injector cones, springs, piston rings, and take a justifiable pride in their self-sufficiency. The clean, slightly acid hill water needs no treatment and boiler life is excellent. Copper tubes last 12 years, and the Sharp Stewart built in 1889 was re-boilered in 1924, and is still in first-class condition.

These little locomotives are almost indestructible. Utterly simple, with boilers pressed to 160 lb/sq in, two 11in × 14in outside cylinders and flat slide valves with Walschaerts gear, they take a terrific pounding and are always ready for more. Of the 29 not more than two are normally out of service and once in the shops they are out again in 18 days after having the boiler off and the axles dropped.

Equally a part of the scene are the train crews. Stocky, ever cheerful, hard-working hill tribesmen, they belong to their railway and it to them. Built up from tradition and experience their train working is a joy, with every man of the five or six in an engine crew knowing his part, from sanding from the front buffer beam to driving; with the train crew operating the brakes on each carriage or wagon with inter-communication by the whistle cord which extends the length of the train along the roof. Moving on after an excellent lunch at the PWD bungalow at Tindaria, I was ushered into the splendid Victorian bogie observation saloon — resplendent in its blue livery with cut-glass lampshades, polished brass fittings and carved teak pillars, furnished with leather 'club' furniture with immaculate white drill covers and a bearer to attend to the material needs of life. What a way to go train recording!

Specially attached to the tail of a freight train — a fish special I suspect — we pulled out of Tindaria at 1500hrs on the haul up to Ghoom — highest point on the line (7,407ft) before the final drop to Darjeeling (6,812ft). One of the toughest sections on the railway is the haul up from Darjeeling to Ghoom — on the return journey before the run down to the plain. Just before Ghoom is the famous double loop at Basatia where in two superimposed spirals the track rises 187ft and the sight and sound of two trains in convoy, struggling up on the limit of adhesion with the blast echoing off the hills, is something never to be forgotten. One of my fonder memories of this railway is breakfast at Kurseong. Here in the station, the morning train from Darjeeling to Siliguri pauses for an engine change during which passengers may breakfast in the restaurant which has never lost its Victorian aura. Normally, the guard rounds up his flock before proceeding, but on one occasion I and my two companions were devouring our scrambled eggs and coffee, when we espied our train departing. Much shouting and yelling, and the train stopped in the High Street whilst we, downing coffee, grabbing cameras, and handing out money, set off in pursuit. Boarding the train to the accompaniment of some good-natured badinage, we experienced the ultimate courtesy when a panting bearer arrived and proffered our change on a tray through the window. But to me, the queen of them all is the little 2ft 0in gauge Matheran railway. Matheran (Forest on the top) is an enchanting hill station, some 60 miles by rail from Bombay on the way to Poona. Materan has no access by road. From 1850 when Sir Poyntz Malet, the Collector of Thana, 'discovered' it, until 1907 when Sir Adamjee Peerbhoy founded the Matheran Hill Light Railway Co, it was accessible only by bridle path. Now perched 2,500ft up on one of the dramatic outcrops of the Deccan plateau, you can journey by rail. Catch the 8·55 out of Dadar station in Bombay and leave the train at Neral junction 86 minutes later. Cross the station bridge and pass through the barrier and you may see before you the 603 passenger due to depart at 1100 hrs. You will certainly find a fascinating selection of coaching stock, ranging from the single compartment 8-seat 4-wheelers weighing 2·3 tonnes to an assortment of bogie stock of relatively grand but assorted proportions — all in their smart blue livery. You may also find at least twice as many people on the platform as could conceivably be crammed into a train of 36 tonnes tare — the limit for the track. But this is where the enchantment begins!

Little seems to have been published about this line, so let me describe its salient features. Matheran is some 2,000 odd feet above Neral and, in plan, about four miles to the West. The track winds up its way the contours for 12·6 miles, clinging to a precipitous wooded hillside, twisting and turning as it rounds projecting rock buttresses and the heads of deep ravines. There are 281 curves, hardly any bridges and only one tunnel of 35 metres length curving sharply left as one climbs. At every turn the passenger is surprised by new vistas of the surrounding hills, their rocky peaks for all the world resembling some broken Brobdingnagian battlement.

The motive power provides an interesting contrast between 1907 and 1955. The impressive JUNG Bo-Bo fully articulated double-ended diesels with central cab and Voith transmission provide the modern counterpart to the four 62-year old steamers. These engines, outwardly conventional 24 ton 0-6-0 side tanks with outside frames and motion work and boilers pressed to 180lb/sq in, are perhaps the only extant locomotives in the world working on the priciple of articulation devised (I believe) by Sir Arthur Haywood in about 1870, of which 'River Irt' on the Ravenglass & Eskdale was the prototype, though long since converted to a rigid configuration.

The last time I passed through the barrier an enormous school outing from Bombay had already packed the train to double its capacity. A diesel was at the head and prospects of my first-class reservation were remote. I need not have worried; along came the guard saying, apologetically, that he was organising a relief train in half-an-hour and would see that my seat was vacated. 'Is there likely to be a steam loco on the relief' I enquired, adding that if there were, I would wait for it and the present trainload could be left undisturbed. 'No, sir — but if you would prefer steam, I'll arrange it, and you would probably like a spell on the footplate too.' So out came No 740, and with much manual pushing and shunting a collection of stock was assembled to form the relief train with one of the little 4-wheel single compartment first class coaches reserved for me to retire to if the footplate became untenable, which — needless to say — it did not. Tradition, friendliness and courtesy — but so it is all over this great railway system where they are still building steam and maintaining and operating 80-year-olds which exhibit all the signs of perennial youth.

Above left: Here is a North Western Railway scene on the 2ft 6in gauge Kalka Simla Railway with up goods train near Salogra, hauled by Kitson Meyer 2-6-2 + 2-6-2 articulated tank engine.

Above: The North Western Railway on the 2ft 6in gauge Kangra Valley Railway with the down train arriving at Jawalimukhi Road behind G class 2-8-2.

Far left: A view of a Western Railway train on bridge No 104 between Bilimora and Waghai, on the narrow gauge 2ft 6in section.

Left: The Kalka Simla Railway was an attractive mountain line, though not quite so precipitous as the Darjeeling Railway. Before diesel haulage, it was the abode of some attractive sturdy tank engines with long water tanks extending right forward to the smokebox. Here is a picture at Dharampur Station.

Above left: The partition of India which formed Pakistan found the 2ft 6in gauge line from Kalabagh to Bannu in Pakistan territory. Here is a train from Bannu crossing the Indus bridge to Kalabagh en route to Mari Indus. The truck in front of the locomotive is there to explode mines in the event of sabotage.

Above: In India metre gauge lines are to be found almost everywhere, and indeed metre gauge lines at 15,600 miles just about equal the total mileage of broad gauge 5ft 6in. Many metre gauge and broad gauge locomotives have been built in India since the war and here is one of the standard metre gauge Pacifics of the YP class on the Western Railway at the Delhi Serai Rohilla station at the head of a train of thirteen coaches.

Far left: A highly local line on the 2ft 6in gauge can be found on the outskirts of Delhi in the Shahdara Saharanpur Light Railway which runs across the flat farmlands for 40 or 50 miles. The locomotives are 2-6-2 and 2-6-4 Hunslet tank engines and here is one of them at Delhi Shahdara station.

Left: The authors got lost here as the location and ownership of this small Garratt escaped us. However we liked the picture and have therefore included it.

Above: Running down the hill towards Darjeeling from the summit 4½ miles away at Ghum is a train on the Darjeeling 2ft gauge railway. At the head end is one of the standard 0-4-0 saddle tank engines which do such sturdy work on this line and which normally carry a crew of six; there also seem to be a couple of Gurkha soldiers on board, one riding between the first and second cars and one on the tail end. An older form of transport is coming up the hill.

Above right: On the Darjeeling Railway, the train is about to leave Siliguri, its terminus at the head of the Indian plains. There seems to be a good load on board and the locomotive crew have got a big stack of coal to ferry the little train with its overflow of passengers up the hill to the summit at Ghum, a climb of 6,600ft in 47 miles.

Right: Back on the Kalka Simla line, we can show one of the 2-6-2 tank engines with the big side tanks, this one with Caprotti valve gear. Alas, these handsome locomotives are no longer in service.

Below: A modern ZP class 2-6-2 built by Henschel for the metre gauge lines of the South Eastern Railway. This is one of the standard passenger locomotives which was used for metre gauge service in India until the arrival after the war of the more powerful Yp Pacifics.

Right: There were some very busy 2ft 6in gauge lines in the outskirts of Calcutta on the north side of the river. The Howrah-Amta and the Howrah-Sheakhala covered a fantastic number of passengers between them over 61 miles of track. Here is a train on the Howrah Amta line with one of the multitude of 0-4-2 tank engines at Bankra.

Far right: ''The public be damned!'' Here is a typical rush hour scene on the Howrah-Amta line in the outskirts of Calcutta.

Below: The Nilgiri Hills rise out of the baking plains of Southern India to a height of over 7,000ft. Here, at all times of the year, the little resort town of Ootacamund is delightfully cool and indeed in our experience can be downright cold after dark. Ootacamund is served by a metre gauge line, part of which runs on the rack from Mettupalaiyam in the plains below. The big 0-8-2 rack and adhesion engines run constantly on the downhill side of the train pushing from the back on the ascent and leading the way going down. The locomotives are an attractive bright Cambridge blue in colour and give an enjoyable footplate ride.

Below right: Here is an attractive red 2-6-4 tank engine on the southern lines in Madras Province. The origin is unknown but it looks like a Kitson to us. One very like it but rather smaller acts as a fussy station pilot at Mettupalaiyam at the foot of the line up to the Nilgiris.

বাঁকড়া
BANKRA বাঁকড়া

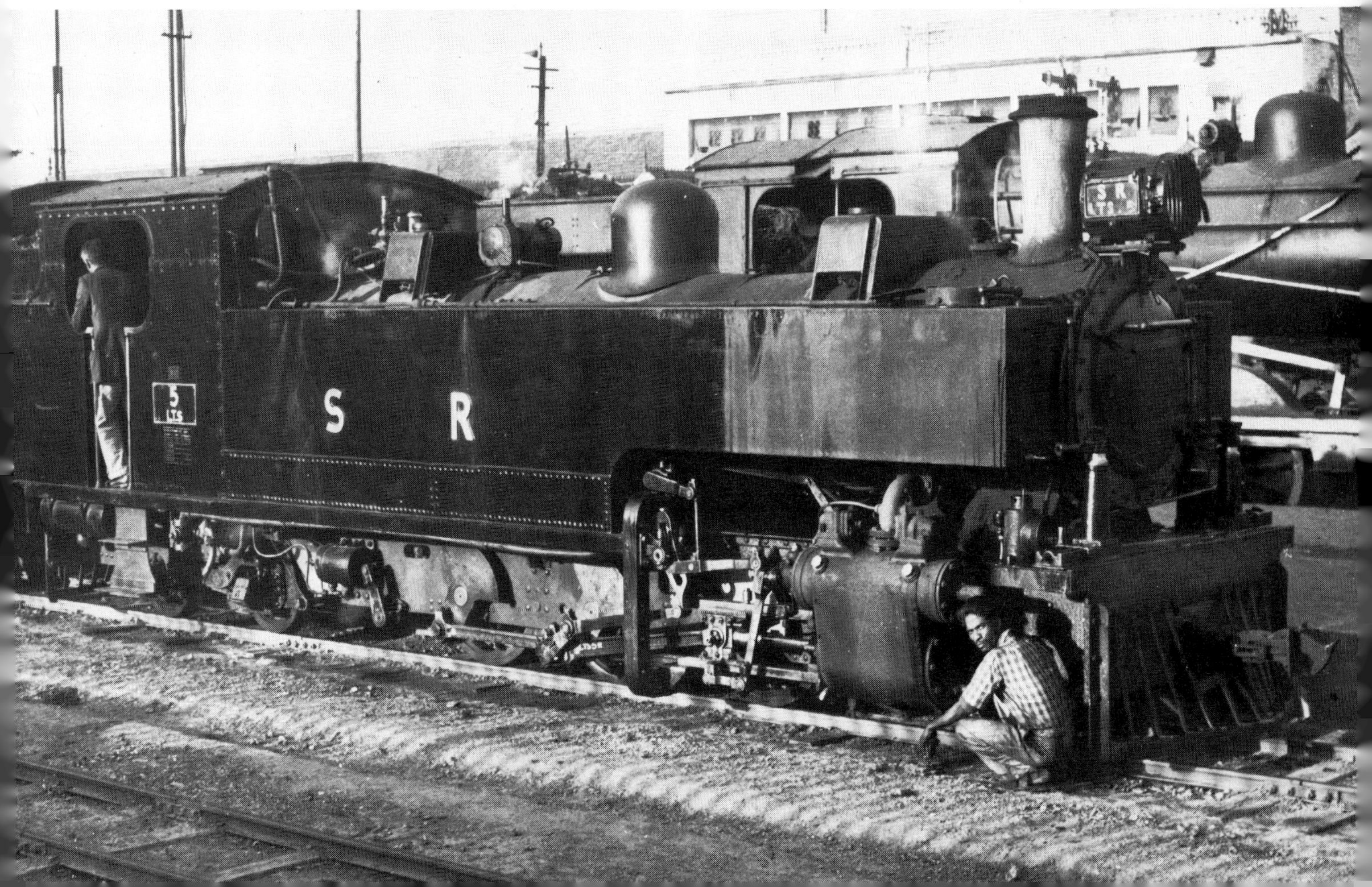

NEPAL

The independent kingdom of Nepal has a short railway system running from Raxaul to Amelkhganj. The line is mostly confined to the Terai, a strip of jungle full of wild beasts of great ferocity, and does not go very far into the Himalayan foothills. The locomotive is 2ft 6in gauge 0-6-2 tank engine No 3 built by Avonside, and the train is the daily Raxaul to Amelkhganj passenger train.

THAILAND
ศาลาแม่ทา
SALA MAE THA
914
914

Right: The railways of Siam or Thailand were well worth a visit while steam still survived and the engines were usually most beautifully kept. Many of the steam engines were built in Japan. Here is a Pacific built after World War II at the Makkasan shop in Bangkok in 1969.

Below: This is another Japanese engine on the Thailand Railways with a mixed train from Chiang Mai to Nakon Lampang, stopping at Sala Mae Tha. The engine is a 2-8-2, No 914.

Right: A Japanese 4-6-2 built for the Thailand Railways by Nippon Sharyo at Nagoya in 1950. The locomotive is a rare thing for these days, a wood burner. The picture was taken in 1962 at Bangkok.

JAPAN

Above left: Steam has gone now in Japan, but in its day the 3ft 6in gauge lines of the JNR had many classes of steam engines and some very powerful machines. The biggest passenger engines were the C62s, 4-6-4s which had many interchangeable parts with the most powerful freight engines, 2-8-2s and 2-8-4s. Here is a group of C62s on shed.

Above: Typically Japanese mountain scenery. The picture shows a small freight train on the main island behind a 2-8-2.

Left: As always the little old engines ended up on the branch lines and here is an ancient Mogul on the Kōmi line at Nobeyama as late as 1958.

Below: This photograph shows the difficult country through which so many miles of the Japanese National Railways network operates. A comparatively small freight train requires banking and the 2-8-0 on the front seems to be getting some powerful assistance.

Above: A double-headed express in hilly country north of Tokyo, with two C62 4-6-4s on the front end. These big engines were the most powerful in the fleet and ran all over the main islands. Japanese Railways had a total of over 12,000 miles of 3ft 6in gauge.

Right: Here is another rather charming little freight, this time behind a Pacific of the C58 class.

These engines were originally built for main line passenger service before being superseded by bigger engines or by electrification.

Below: This is a very unusual angle of two of the largest Pacifics of the JNR with a passenger train in the hills of Honshu. This picture, although taken in 1960, really shows a bygone age.

Below right: Here is a rather forlorn little 2-4-2 tank engine once on the JNR but later on the Jobu Railway. One's immediate response to this is to think of the Cork Blackrock and Passage Railway in Ireland which had a fleet of engines of 3ft gauge very like this one, and indeed this Japanese engine may well have been built in Britain.

PHILIPPINES

Below: At the end of the war the Philippine Railways were in bad shape and all kinds of improvisations had to make good the shortage of locomotives. The Manila Railway on the island of Luzon ran on the 3ft 6in gauge and just after the war had some steam survivors in service. Here is a three cylinder, oil-burning Pacific on an afternoon express from Manila leaying Dau Station.

Left: Here is another huge chimney locomotive on the Manila Railway in the island of Luzon. The locomotive here is an Atlantic with a local passenger train. These engines have long since disappeared. The Philippine Railways will probably repay study as the local lines, many of which were built for carrying sugar cane, apparently had some remarkable motive power. Indeed, the comparatively small island of Negros had no fewer than twelve separate railways and gauges ranging from 2ft to 4ft 8½in. These burned bagasse or sugar cane waste which necessitated a roof over the tender.

SOUTH VIETNAM

Left: Here is a 1969 picture from Vietnam showing a special passenger train from Saigon to Bien Hoa with the General Electric diesel pushing two flat cars for protection against mines. Also in the train is an armoured car carrying soldiers. The photograph was taken near Thu Duc.

Above: The Vietnam Railways, which, of course, were horribly knocked about in recent years, include a rack section from Song Pha to Dalat on the metre gauge. This is 0-8-0 rack-and-adhesion tank engine No 40-303 on the 12 per cent grade out of Song Pha to El Gio.

MALAYA

Above: The beautiful steam engines which were so clean and admirably kept still survive in limited numbers we hope; here is one of them in the shape of 56 class Pacific leaving Prai in North Malaya in front of a well polished passenger train.

Above right: O class Pacific No 564.13 leaving Singapore with the evening mixed train for Kuala Lumpur in the sixties. This locomotive was one of a group of 40 built in 1946 by the North British Locomotive Company. They are three-cylinder machines with rotary cam poppet valve gear.

Below: The Malayan Railways at Singapore. I class 0-6-4 tank engine No 301.15 shunting at Tanglin Halt. These British engines were built by Hawthorn Leslie & Co during World War I.

Right: The causeway linking the mainland with Singapore Island carries a road, a railway and a huge water pipe for Singapore city. Here is the night mail from Kuala Lumpur running over the causeway to Singapore in the days of steam. This is a big express for the metre gauge with fifteen cars painted in Great Western chocolate and cream with a bright green, oil-burning Pacific at the head.

56413

INDONESIA/NORTH BORNEO

Top: The Dutch built a network of railways in Indonesia, particularly in Java, on the 3ft 6in gauge, although some of the minor lines built are narrower than this. 'In the good old days' some fast express running was carried out and some very lively 4-6-4 well tank engines did much of this work. These engines still survive in active service.

Above: This is a Mallet tank engine on the Java State Railways, photographed in 1960. This 2-6-6-0 was built in Dutch colonial days by the Nederlandshe Fabrik at Amsterdam in 1911.

Right: Here is a mixed steam train on the North Borneo Railways on the 100 mile line which runs into the interior from Jesselton through the picturesque Tenom Gorge. The line is particularly used for rubber, timber and other freight. The locomotive, we would guess, is a Vulcan Foundry or Armstrong Whitworth 2-8-2.

TURKEY

Right: There is a small section of 2ft 6in gauge line in Turkey running inland from Samsun on the Black Sea coast. Here is 2-6-0 tank No 34801 approaching Samsun along the Black Sea coast with a train from Carsamba. This is the only passenger narrow gauge service operated by the Turkish Railways. The picture was taken in September 1968.

Below: Here is another view on the Turkish narrow gauge line at Carsamba with 2-6-0 tank No 34801 having arrived with the afternoon train from Samsun.

IRAQ/JORDAN

Below: The former Chemin de Fer de Damas, Hama et Prolongements was originally built to connect Beirút with Syria and then on down to Damascus and on through Deraa to Jordan and Medina in the desert. The line is now split between the various countries and operating through the most interesting and arduous section is that in the Lebanon which has many miles on the Abt rack system. A variety of locomotives work on this and here is a big Swiss-built 0-10-0 tank with a special train conveying skiers up from Beirút to the Lebanon mountains. The rack section starts almost in the city of Beirút itself.

Top right: A big 2-8-4 tank engine of the Iraq Petroleum Company after some repairs at Baghdad workshops. Baghdad is served by both metre and standard gauge, but this is a metre gauge engine. The fireman is taking advantage of the shade.

Middle right: The Jordan Railways, running on the 105cm gauge, are a continuation of the Hedjaz Railway originally built by Turkey in the Near East, the remains of which are also found in Syria and the Lebanon. The principal line in Jordan runs down parallel to the river but well to the east of it from Damascus through 'Amman and on down through to the little town of Ma'an. A variety of elderly locomotives run this line. Here is a Hartman 2-8-2 built for the Turks in 1918.

Bottom right: Also on the Hedjaz Railway, here is another locomotive, this one an 0-6-0 shown here with an auxiliary tank taken at 'Amman. This line originally ran right down to Medina through the desert but, although there is the intention to repair this section, the line has taken years to recover from the depredations of Colonel T. E. Lawrence's irregulars in World War I.

PRIORITY
TRAFFIC
NO SMOKING
SICARA İÇİLMEZ
MH KAΠNIZETE

Below: The Cyprus Government Railway. Here is a small 2ft 6in gauge 4-4-0 on a mixed freight and passenger train at Famagusta in 1948. This little line barely survived the war.

Right: The Cyprus Mining Corporation had some fine yellow steam engines for hauling their ore out from the mines to shipment. Here is one of these, an 0-8-2 tank built by Baldwin in 1928.

The Pacific

Here is another enormous area but this time almost all water. There is little new to offer here, alas. Steam on the attractive sugar lines of Fiji has disappeared, though we are glad to record some pictures from its heyday.

Steam, too, has gone from the Hawaiian Islands, indeed it barely survived World War II, although it produced some attractive pictures.

We're afraid that we have no knowledge of possible mineral or phosphate rock carriers in Nauru but New Caledonia has just been reported on by Charles Small in his excellent *Rails to the Setting Sun*; only wreckage remains.

Australia, of course, is a big narrow gauge territory outside of New South Wales, Victoria and South Australia. Queensland has always had a 3ft 6in gauge state system, apart from its 1,000 miles of 2ft sugar railways, now dieselised. Western Australia has also 3ft 6in gauge as its standard, but now the 4ft 8½in has thrust through to Perth from Kalgoorlie to make it possible to travel in one train from Sydney to Perth for the first time. Indeed, as a fine gesture, this was done recently by a steam hauled train in a triumphant tour behind NSW Pacific No 3801.

Some steam survives in Western Australia as the result of a policy of maintaining steam reserves, as it does in Queensland, but not very much and there it has a decidedly limited prospect.

In Victoria the 'Puffing Billy' 2ft 6in gauge line in the Dandenong Hills east of Melbourne goes from strength to strength, with now four of the little sturdy 2-6-2 tanks in service.

On the whole though, Australia in 1972 was rather a sad place for the steam enthusiast and there seemed to be too much in museums, good as they were, and too little in service.

New Zealand, 'steamwise', is much the same, all gone on the Government Railways in the north island, and almost all in the south, though we did spot an industrial tank engine in the suburbs of Auckland on our way to pay homage to the great 4-8-4 No 800 on its plinth at the steelworks in 1971. On the other hand, a live museum is starting life in Auckland, and offered us a chance to ride and drive a little Andrew Barclay 0-4-0 tank with a sharp beat, though on a most restricted run.

We feel we are lucky in having so many pictures of the heyday of steam in New Zealand so admirably done for us by Derek Cross.

97
AUSTRALIAN
RAILWAY
HISTORICAL SOCIETY
GLADSTONE
TO
WILMINGTON
6-5-62

AUSTRALIA

Above: Australia was excellent territory for the narrow gauge enthusiast because, apart from the state railways of New South Wales which throughout were built to 4ft 8½in, there was narrow gauge in every state and even New South Wales had the Silverton Tramway. The whole of Queensland was on 3ft 6in gauge until the standard gauge came creeping over the frontier to link Brisbane with Sydney, and some powerful attractive steam engines were built for the Queensland lines. Here is a QGR Pacific of class BB18¼ undergoing some minor repairs at Mayne Road Depot, Brisbane in 1960. The Queensland engines were always nicely kept and the express engines had green painted boilers, while the suburban tank engines were painted a bright light blue.

Above right: South Australia like Victoria was originally laid out by Irish engineers and its main lines were built to 5ft 3in gauge. There was, however, a considerable mileage of 3ft 6in and some of it carried heavy traffic, notably the ore traffic which came down on the Silverton Tramway from Broken Hill by 3ft 6in gauge, to make a junction with the South Australian Railways at Cockburn. From there down to Port Pirie the ore trains were usually hauled by some powerful 4-8-2 + 2-8-4 Garratts, of which one is shown here at Cockburn. These engines were built to be capable of being converted to 4ft 8½in or 5ft 3in gauge.

Below: Here is an Australian Railway Historical Society 'special' train near Melrose, South Australia, on one of the 3ft 6in lines of the South Australian Railways. At the head is a small Y class 2-6-0, built in 1890 by Beyer Peacock, with a quite inordinately large dome, while the train engine is T class 4-8-0 built in 1917.

Right: Also in South Australia are the private lines of the Broken Hill Proprietary Company who run a 3ft 6in gauge line known as the Whyalla & Iron Knob Tramway. The Australian Railway Historical Society are enjoying a ride here in 1964 behind the last steam survivor on this line, 4-6-0 No 4, built by Baldwin in 1914.

405
405

MURCHISON

Cascade

Above left: Tasmania is in many ways one of the most attractive states in Australia. Not only does it provide a lot of beautiful scenery but some very wild and strange country as well, particularly on the western coast where there is an inordinate rainfall and temperate rain forest in consequence. On account of the minerals found in this wild country, railways forced their way through and the Emu Bay line running south from Burnie still survives to operate such minor traffic as offers. For a time in the early sixties, the Emu Bay was also running a passenger service to fit in with a tour company and for this purpose put on a very attractive train called the 'West Coaster' behind specially painted 4-8-0 locomotives. Here is No 6 *Murchison* heading the 'West Coaster' at Rosebery. The engine is an attractive Caledonian blue with a lighter paint along the running board and the coaches are in two shades of blue. The picture was taken in 1960.

Above: During World War II the Australian Government ordered the construction of a number of Garratts for 3ft 6in gauge work. These were built by several makers and were known as the Australian Standard Garratt. Here is one on the Emu Bay Railway in Tasmania at Farrell, heading a goods train.

Left: Further south in Tasmania the Mt Lyell Mining and Railway Company worked a 3ft 6in gauge line down to the coast from the copper ore mines of Queenstown. This line has now been superseded by road transport but in its day ran with a group of five 0-4-2 rack-and-adhesion locomotives, the most recent of which is the one shown here, built in 1938. The rack section was about five miles long and this, of course, is what really killed the railway.

213

Left: The Commonwealth Railways of Australia are known particularly for their transcontinental line built during World War I, connecting Kalgoorlie to Port Pirie Junction on 4ft 8½in gauge. This line has been extended at each end so that a continuous run from Sydney to Perth is now possible. The Commonwealth Railways also ran a 3ft 6in branch to Alice Springs in Central Australia, which at one time was intended to reach all the way to Darwin in the northern territories. Here is a Central Australian Railway motor train preserved at Alice Springs. This little train once ran on the Quorn-Hawker branch of the South Australian Railways in the Flinders Ranges.

Above: Apart from the Commonwealth Railways standard gauge line into Kalgoorlie and then the extension continued through to Perth and Fremantle in the last few years, the Western Australian Railways were all built for the 3ft 6in gauge. The locomotives were painted green and were usually well kept into the bargain. Here is a goods train northbound near Pingelly in 1962, double-headed with two Pacifics.

Below left: Narrow gauge in Victoria consisted of several little 2ft 6in gauge lines of which only one survives, namely, the holiday and tourist line in the Dandenong Hills, east of Melbourne, where the 'Puffing Billy' service thrives especially on summer weekends. This line is served by four 2-6-2 tank engines of a Baldwin design, one of which was from its original makers and the other made from the same drawings in the Victorian Railways' shops at Newport. The picture shows the train in its earlier days leaving Upper Ferntree Gully for Belgrave. This line has since been widened and electrified, but 'Puffing Billy' has pushed further into the forests from Belgrave up to Emerald.

Below middle: 'Puffing Billy' seems to have a load on here, though personally we would doubt whether she ever actually went up the hill quite as full as this. Nonetheless, on the Sunday on which we rode the footplate, the train was very well patronised and the ride was both spectacular and attractive through thick woods full of cicadas and bell-birds.

Below: We have no information about this picture except that it shows the Dandenong Hills line with 'Puffing Billy' hard at work.

Above left: This photograph was taken in the centre of North Island and shows the midday goods train from Frankton to Kinleith near Lichfield in the spring of 1957. The train is on a 1 in 50 bank and is hauled by K class oil-fired 4-8-4 No 913, assisted by a 4-6-4 tank engine of Class Wab. The New Zealand Railways, like the old Great Western, usually put the assisting locomotive behind the train engine.

Top: The New Zealand Army built a camp at Waiouru, on the moors about 2,500ft up, close to the main Wellington/Auckland line in the North Island. The camp was served by a short branch and the picture shows the daily goods train from the camp to Waiouru in March 1957, crossing the main road hauled by a dwarf Fowler 0-4-0 well-tank. This locomotive was formerly used in construction work in various places and was one of a fleet of small engines used by the Public Works Department.

Above: In 1954 steam was going strong all over New Zealand and the picture here shows the running shed at Auckland in that year. The locomotives visible are the coal-burning J class 4-8-2 No 1220 and oil-burning Ja class 4-8-2 No 1282 and Ab class Pacific No 823.

Far left: A Frankton-Kinleith goods half a mile from the junction with the Rotorua line at Putaruru heading for the newly developed pine forests and mills at Kinleith. On May 19th 1956 the midday train from Putaruru is hauled by J class 4-8-2 No 1235 (coal-burner) piloting oil-burning K class 4-8-4 No 928

Left: Royal trains are always good fun and New Zealand is no exception to this. The picture shows a double-headed train with two Ab class Pacifics at Cross Creek, the foot of the Rimutaka Incline, during the 1954 Royal Tour.

Far top left: The Rimutaka Incline was an irresistible attraction until it closed down in October 1955 when the new 5½ mile tunnel was opened. For years this line was faithfully served by six 0-4-2 tank engines with the Fell centre rail. This picture shows the locomotive depot at Cross Creek on a Sunday morning with four of the locomotives receiving attention from two of the shed staff and three dogs. A happy rural scene.

Left: We are still on the Rimutaka Incline: five Fell engines, having just worked a train up the 1 in 15 grade, are returning light (with four of the special Fell brake vans). The area besides being mountainous was exposed to furious winds and rainstorms, and protective fences were erected in places along the line.

Far middle left: Often enough three, four or even five of the Fell engines worked together on one train on the Rimutaka Incline.

Below left: For 30 or 40 miles out of Wellington the main line north to Auckland in the North Island runs on a fairly narrow strip between the hills and the sea. This picture shows the Wellington-Auckland express train No 626 in September 1955 headed by two oil-fired Ka class 4-8-4s Nos 933 and 958.

Below: Derek Cross is a highly expert photographer with an eye for the unusual and lowly as well as the great and magnificent. Here is one of his minor train studies, the Greymouth to Rewanui mine train carrying goods and empty coal wagons in 1955. The tank engine is We class No 377. This line had a Fell section on which the centre rail was used only for braking. The locomotive illustrated has, therefore, a special movable flap in the centre of the cow-catcher which can be lifted to clear the Fell line.

FIJI

Above left: The Monday and Thursday Mba (pronounced Baa)-Lautoka free passenger train hauled by Hudswell Clarke 4-4-0 No 18 climbing out of the Mba Valley some five miles on its way to Lautoka in September 1958. The appearance of the photographer for a second time in quick succession has had a very stirring effect on the passengers! In view of the importance of the job the 4-4-0 was spared the coal/cane waste mixture and so the smoke has a conventional appearance. By the way, as Lautoka/Mba was only 25 miles each way the passenger job was on an out-and-back-in-the-day basis but the Tuesday and Friday run to Singatoka on the south coast was too long for one day out and back so they went down on Tuesdays and Fridays and came back the following day. The ride was free.

Above: Four little engines sheltering from the heat of the day under a huge flame tree in the cane fields near Nandi waiting to work their loaded cane trains back to the Lautoka mill in the evening. These are all Hudswell Clarke 0-6-0s numbered 24, 22, 25 and 21 in order from the front. Derek Cross writes ''When I saw this in September 1958 I had to walk for about half a mile up a very dusty track as my Indian taxi driver refused point blank to go any nearer as the place was known as 'Wailing Ghost Gully'. Where the loco crews were I don't know . . . perhaps the ghosts had got them but I was very tempted to couple them up and take them away!''

Left: Fowler 0-6-2T No 9 at the head of an empty cane train at Nandi in September 1958.

Below: The Mba-Lautoka passenger train with Hudswell Clarke 4-4-0 No 18 in charge pictured 12 miles south of Alba in September 1958.

HAWAII

Left: On the main island of Oahu in the Hawaiian group there was a considerable railway system just after World War II before a hurricane and tidal wave did away with much of it. Now there is a small surviving line which serves the pineapple and cane fields near Honolulu. Here is a double-headed goods train in the 1940s, eastbound for Waipahu from the Wahiawa branch and Dole siding.

Above: This system on the 3ft gauge was on the island of Maui and the Kahului Railroad was one of the last 3ft gauge common carriers in the United States. Here is No 12 of Kahului Railway in the yards, an attractive little 2-6-2 with a semi cylindrical water tank built by Baldwin.

223

Photo Credits

John Adams: 157(B)
Albrekt: 54(B)
Peter Allen: 12(T), 57(B), 96(B), 120(B), 121(B), 123, 124(B), 125(T), 131(T) 131(M), 132, 133(B), 143(B), 145(B), 146, 147, 163, 167, 171(T), 206, 210(T) 211(T), 212(T), 213(T), 214(T)
T. E. Attié: 204
Authors' Collection: 55, 82(T), 103(B), 124(T), 126, 178(B), 182(B), 183, 184(T), 185(B), 190(T), 198(T), 199(B), 205(M), 205(B), 215(BR)
Nic Badenhorst: 155(T)
Frank Barry: 142(B), 144, 145(T)
Murray Befeler (of Hawaii): 223
Benguela Railway: 164(T), 165
P. S. A. Berridge: 178(T), 179(T), 180(T)
Gerald M. Best: 106(B), 139(B), 140(B), 142, 189(B), 200(B), 215(T),
Lt Edward N. Bewlay: 194, 195(I)
J. D. Blythe: 40(T)
S. K. Bolton (by permission of Rail Photo Service): 111(B)
James I. C. Boyd: 20(T)
British Information Services: 170(B), 171(B), 201
Canadian National Railways: 100
CFM Official: 162(T)
D. J. Colquhoun: 211(B), 214(B)
G. C. Corey (by permission of Rail Photo Service): 112(B)
Major E. A. S. Cotton: 198(B), 199(T)
R. B. Crane: 139(T)
Derek Cross: 13(B), 14(B), 22(T), 38(T), 181(B), 186, 216, 217, 218, 219, 220, 221
Gordon Crowell: 128, 129
B. F. Cutler (by permission of Rail Photo Service): 110(B)
J. G. Dewing: 22(B), 25(B)
A. E. Durrant: 160
East African Railways: 168(T), 169(T)
Eastern Railway, Calcutta: 179(B)
Oscar Elsden: 43(I), 120(T), 122(T), 170(T)
M. O. England: 11(B), 94, 95, 96(T), 97
R. K. Evans: 28(B), 29B)
Fox Photos Ltd: 182(T)
W. Fritthom: 74(B)
Trevor S. Hamer: 151(T)
L. T. Haug (Collection of Gerald M. Best): 139(M)
Hawaiian Railroads: 222
G. F. Heiron: 172, 173(T)
Herald-Sun, The Herald & Weekly Times: 215(BL)

High Commissioner's Office: 156(B), 159(B)
J. A. Ingram: 12(B)
Walter Jack: 210(B)
JNR Official: 191, 192(T)
A. A. Jorgensen: 151(B), 152(T), 153, 154(T), 163(B), 164(B)
Kenya Information Services: 168(B)
D. W. Koch: 37(B)
J. Langham: 205(T), 207(I)
O. Winthur Laursen: 48, 50, 51(B), 52, 53(B), 54(T), 56(T), 57(T), 58(T), 61, 62, 64, 66(T), 67(T)
H. Le Fleming: 200(T)
Charles Lewis: 150(T)
Jack Lindsay: 127(T)
Ed Lohr (Gerald M. Best Collection): 138(B)
Robert Lorenz (by permission of Rail Photo Service): 112(T)
Alfred Luft: 46(T), 47(T), 70, 75(B), 76, 79(T), 80, 82(B), 83(B)
P. J. Lynch: 23
Lawrence Marshall: 53(T), 90(M), 90(B), 92, 93
M. Mensing: 15
H. Michimura: 190(B), 193(B)
Paul Morby: 75(T)
Saburo Motojima: 192(B), 193(T)
Carl E. Mulvihill: 103(T)
Harald Navé: 33, 38(B), 39, 42, 44(T), 49(B), 68, 90(T) 91(B)
L. A. Nixon: 86, 87, 88(T), 89(T)
H. S. Patrick: 130, 131(B)
D. L. Percival: 17
L. W. Perkins: 18(T)
Ivo Peters: 10, 14(T), 25(T)
H. W. Pontin (by permission of Rail Photo Service): 114(T)
P. Ransome-Wallis: 77(I), 101(B)
John A. Rehor (J. William Vigrass Collection): 101(T)
D. Trevor Rowe: 28(T), 30(T), 40(B), 41(B), 51(T), 56(B), 58(B), 59(B), 60(B), 66(B), 67(B), 72, 73, 74(T), 78, 85(B), 118, 119, 125(B), 133(T)
D. Trevor Rowe (by permission of Robert Spark): 84 (T)
E. S. Russell: 34
SAR Official: 150(B), 152(B), 154(B), 155(B)
M. G. Satow: 184
Jim Shaughnessy: 104, 105, 106(T), 107, 114(B), 115, 134, 135, 136, 137, 138(T), 140(T), 141
Charles S. Small: 162(B), 212(B)
Southern Pacific Historical Collection: 110(T), 111(T)
The Statesman: 185(T)
Paul S. Stephanus: 81(T), 113, 180(B), 181(T), 188, 189(T), 196, 197
Ray E. Tobey (by permission of Rail Photo Service): 114(M)
Peter Waugh: 166
P. B. Whitehouse: 11(T), 15(T), 16(TR), 16(B), 19(T), 18(B), 20(B), 21, 24(T), 31, 36(B), 41(T), 84(B), 108, 109, 169(M), 169(M)
P. B. Whitehouse Collection: 19(B), 30(B), 32
C. M. Whitehouse: 158, 159(T)
White Pass and Yukon Railway: 102(B)
Daniel H. Wilson: 16(TL)
D. W. Winkworth: 13(T), 29(T), 35, 36(T), 44(B), 45, 48(B), 49(I), 81(B), 83(T), 85(T), 90(B), 91(BT), 202, 203(I)